H. P. B.

REBIRTH OF THE OCCULT TRADITION

How the Secret Doctrine of
H. P. Blavatsky Was Written

BORIS DE ZIRKOFF

*(Historical Introduction to the Two-Volume 1978 Edition of
The Secret Doctrine)*

THE THEOSOPHICAL PUBLISHING HOUSE
Adyar Madras 600 020 India
Wheaton, Ill., U.S.A. • London, England

Reprint 1990

ISBN : 0-8356-7535-1

Printed at the Vasanta Press
The Theosophical Society
Adyar, Madras 600 020, India.

REBIRTH OF THE OCCULT TRADITION

HOW 'THE SECRET DOCTRINE' OF H. P. BLAVATSKY WAS WRITTEN

The epoch-making work known as *The Secret Doctrine* is the *magnum opus* of Helena Petrovna Blavatsky. Its subtitle is: 'The Synthesis of Science, Religion, and Philosophy'.

The First Volume of *The Secret Doctrine* came off the Press on 20 October 1888. This fact is recorded by Richard Harte, then in London, and about to leave for India. In a set of the original edition (first printing), now in the archives of the present writer, there is, on the half-title page, a note in blue pencil signed by Richard Harte, which says:

> 'This is the first copy ever issued. I got it from Printer by special Messenger on the morning of the 20 Oct. '88 as I was leaving the house 17 Lansdowne Road, with Col. Olcott for India (Col. went personally via Naples). The Second Vol. followed me to India.
>
> R.H.'

The Second Volume of H.P.B.'s *magnum opus* was published either at the end of December 1888, or in January 1889.

Both volumes are bound in light grey. Facing the title-page, there appears the statement: 'Printed by Allen, Scott and Co., 30 Bouverie Street, E.C.'; while the reverse of the title page bears the words:
'Entered at Stationers' Hall. All Rights Reserved.'[1]

The first steps in the writing of what later became known as *The Secret Doctrine* were taken much earlier than most students realize.

---

[1] Copies which were sent to W.Q. Judge in New York were bound in dark blue and bear on the reverse of the title page the words: 'Entered according to Act of Congress in the year 1888 by H.P. Blavatsky, in the Office of the Librarian of Congress at Washington, D.C.'

H.P.B. and Col. Henry S. Olcott had gone to India and had settled for the time being in Bombay. The Colonel was continuing his well-established habit of writing down in his diary succinct statements about various events taking place from day to day. By consulting at a later date his *Diaries* for 1879, he noticed:

> .... several entries about helping H.P.B. to write 'her new book on Theosophy' On 23rd May, it seems, she 'broke ground' for it; on the 24th I 'gave her, by request, the skeleton outline of a book embodying such crude ideas as suggested themselves to one who did not intend to be the writer of it'; on the 25th I 'helped in preparing the Preface'; on 4th of June we finished it; and that seed lay in the mummy's hand five or six years before it sprouted as *The Secret Doctrine*, for which the only thing I then did was to invent the title and write the original Prospectus. After coming to Bombay I had quite enough common routine work to do without helping to write another book of cyclopaedic bulk.[2]

Nothing else seems to have been done on the production of this work for some time, as both Founders were extremely busy establishing their Headquarters in India and launching *The Theosophist*.

Almost three years later, namely in August 1882, we find in one of the Letters from Master K.H. written to A.P. Sinnett, a casual remark made by the writer to the effect that '.... it [Isis] really ought to be *re-written* for the sake of the family honour'.[3]

In January 1884, the Supplement to *The Theosophist*, which began to be issued then under the name of the *Journal of The Theosophical Society* (Vol. I, No. 1), published an advertisement announcing *The Secret Doctrine* and speaking of it as 'A New Version of "Isis Unveiled" '. It read:

> Numerous and urgent requests have come from all parts of India, to adopt some plan for bringing the matter contained in *Isis Unveiled*, within the reach of those who could not afford to purchase so expensive a work at one time. On the other hand, many, finding the outlines of the doctrine given too hazy, clamoured for 'more light', and necessarily misunderstanding the teaching, have erroneously supposed it to be contradictory to later revelations, which in not a few cases, have been entirely misconceived. The author, therefore, under the advice of friends, proposes to issue the work in a better and clearer form, in monthly parts. All that is important in 'Isis' for a thorough comprehension of the occult and other philosophical subjects treated of, will be retained, but with such a rearrangement of the text as to group together as

---

[2] *Old Diary Leaves*, Series II, p. 90.
[3] *The Mahatma Letters to A.P. Sinnett*, Letter No. XXc, p. 130, 3rd rev. ed., p. 127.

closely as possible the materials relating to any given subject. Thus will be avoided needless repetitions, and the scattering of materials of a cognate character throughout the two volumes. Much additional information upon occult subjects, which it was not desirable to put before the public at the first appearance of the work, but for which the way has been prepared by the intervening eight years, and especially by the publication of *The Occult World* and *Esoteric Buddhism* and other Theosophical works, will now be given. Hints will also be found throwing light on many of the hitherto misunderstood teachings found in the said works. A complete Index and a Table of Contents will be compiled. It is intended that each Part shall comprise seventy-seven pages in Royal 8vo. (or twenty-five pages more than every 24th part of the original work) to be printed on good paper and in clear type, and be completed in about two years....

To this was added the rate of subscriptions and directions concerning the remittance of funds, etc.

The February 1884 issue of the *Journal* reprinted the same advertisement and pointed out that this New Version of *Isis Unveiled* would have 'a new arrangement of the matter, large and important additions, and copious Notes and Commentaries, by H.P. Blavatsky, Corresponding Secretary of The Theosophical Society. Assisted by T. Subba Row Garu, B.A., B.L., F.T.S., Councillor of The Theosophical Society and Secretary of its Madras Branch'. The first part was to be 'issued March 15th'. In March, April, and May, the same announcement was repeated, but the date was pushed forward to June 15. In June, July, and August, the date was advanced to August 15.

Similarly, in June 1884, *The Theosophist* (Vol. V, No. 57, p. 232) published a Notice saying:

> We regret to announce that, owing to unavoidable causes, the publication of *The Secret Doctrine* has to be delayed for two months more. The first Number will therefore be out on the 15th of August, instead of 15th of June as originally announced.

In September of the same year, *The Theosophist* inserted the following Notice:

> The delay in the issue of Part I of *The Secret Doctrine* was due to the MSS. not having reached this office in time, from London from Madame Blavatsky, who, besides being in bad health, has a good deal of Society business to do in connection with the European tour. The MSS. have, however, now come and been put into the printer's hand. The first number is expected to be out by the middle of this month. We trust the subscribers will excuse this unavoidable delay of nearly a month.

The September issue of the *Journal of the T.S.* repeated the previous Announcement and gave the date of the 15th of that month as a deadline.

The October issue of *The Theosophist* (Vol.VI, No.61, p.23) came on with a 'Special Notice' which stated that:

> As, in consequence of recent events, Madame Blavatsky's early return to India is expected, it has been decided to postpone the issue of the first part of the 'Secret Doctrine', so as to ensure an uninterrupted succession of numbers after her arrival.
>
> Subscribers are requested to be lenient and have patience, as Madame Blavatsky, besides being in very bad health, has been overwhelmed in Europe with visits and correspondence which have made great inroads upon her time and exhausting drains upon her strength.

The same Notice, together with the earlier Announcement, with no date specified, appeared also in the October issue of the *Journal of the T.S.* (p. 143), and the Announcement alone was printed in the November issue.

In the December issue of *The Theosophist* (Vol. VI, No. 63, p. 74), a Special Notice was published, signed by the President-Founder himself, and dated from Adyar 27 November 1884. It reads:

THE SECRET DOCTRINE: SPECIAL NOTICE

> For the information of friends who have enquired of me personally about the probable time when *The Secret Doctrine* will be issued, the following information is given.
>
> The delays in the appearance of the work have been mainly due to two causes—Mme Blavatsky's almost constant ill-health since her departure for Europe, in February last; and the interference with her literary labours by her travels and official engagements. The paper for the entire edition was purchased several months ago and is at Adyar; the Introduction and First Chapter are in type; and the two volumes of *Isis Unveiled* have been carefully read and annotated for use in the new book. A separate registration is kept of subscribers' names, and their cash remittances amounting to several thousand rupees—are untouched and on special deposit in bank. As Mme Blavatsky is expected at Adyar during the present month, it is hoped and expected that the work will soon appear, and the monthly parts follow each other uninterruptedly.
>
> I therefore invite such as may have been holding back for the issue of the first monthly part, to send in their names as soon as convenient to avoid possible disappointment. The edition to be printed will be limited to the demand and the book will not be stereotyped.

ADYAR   H.S. OLCOTT
27th Nov. 1884

The same Notice appeared in the December issue of the *Journal of the T.S.*

In retrospect, and with many lacunae in the available source-material, it is not easy to determine exactly what was meant by the Manuscripts which had 'now come and been put into the printer's hand'. It is also strange that so much advance publicity had been given to something which, very obviously, was far from being ready and in a rather chaotic state.

Reminiscing about the inception of *The Secret Doctrine*, Dr Archibald Keightley wrote:

> I was told in 1884 that Madame Blavatsky was engaged in writing a book, but I did not know what. Then I heard that the book was to be called *The Secret Doctrine*, that various people had been consulted as to its construction, and that all the moot points of Hindu Philosophy had been submitted to the late T. Subba Row, who had also made various suggestions as to its construction. Afterwards I found that he had done so, sketching out very roughly an outline, but this was not followed.[4]

In the Spring of 1884, William Quan Judge started for India. He arrived in Paris on March 25 and was 'ordered by the Masters to stop here and help Madame [H.P.B.] in writing the "Secret Doctrine" '.[5] This was somewhat in advance of H.P.B.'s arrival, as she and Col. Olcott, coming from India, reached Paris on March 28, and were met there by Mr Judge, Mohini M. Chatterji and Dr Thurmann. On May 13, H.P.B. and Mr Judge went for a visit to Count and Countess Gaston d'Adhémar de Cransac at their 'Château Écossais' situated at Enghien, not far from Paris. In connction with their stay there, Mr Judge wrote:

> At Enghien especially, H.P.B. wanted me to go carefully through the pages of her copy of *Isis Unveiled* for the purpose of noting on the margins what subjects were treated, and for the work she furnished me with what she called a special blue and red pencil. I went all through both volumes and made the notes required, and of those she afterwards wrote me that they were of the greatest use to her.[6]

In a letter written by him to a friend, he also said:

> So then, here I am for how long or short I do not know, and I am to make suggestions and write upon the work. So see my fate again linked with the second working up of 'Isis'. In this place you will remember her letter of last June that my fate was indissolubly linked with that of theirs (the...).

---

[4] Countess C. Wachtmeister, *Reminiscences of H.P. Blavatsky and 'The Secret Doctrine'*, 1893, p. 96.

[5] *The Word*, Vol. XV, April 1912, pp. 17-18.   [6] Wachtmeister, *op.cit.*, p. 102.

> . . . It is quite a task, this selecting and collating from the matter of Isis so that all may be preserved, and, all useless matter expunged.[7]

At approximately the same time, H.P.B. wrote to A.P. Sinnett, on the subject of his forthcoming work, *Esoteric Buddhism*, that she knew it to be based on 'fragments' of Occult Science which were not to be taken for the whole.

> As a whole—*Esoteric Buddhism* cannot of course be considered such, nor have you ever claimed it as far as I know to be the *alpha* and the *omega* of our Doctrine. ... And now the outcome of it is, that I, crippled down and half dead, am to sit up nights again and rewrite the whole of *Isis Unveiled*, calling it *The Secret Doctrine* and making three if not four volumes out of the original two, Subba Row helping me and writing most of the commentaries and explanations.[8]

Writing to A.P. Sinnett on 25 April 1884, H.P.B., then in Paris, spoke at some length about her work on the forthcoming book. She wrote:

> I thank you *for the intention* you had of writing the Preface for *Secret Doctrine*. I did not ask you to do it but the Mahatmas, and Mohini here, and Subba Row *there*, are quite sufficient for the task of helping me. If you *do not* think that 'the scheme is feasible as announced' I am sorry for you and your intuition. Since the Guru thinks it otherwise I will take my chance of following rather his order and advice than yours. This, in sincere friendship, but in as great a determination. To say that I 'would do *wisely* to direct the repayment of subscriptions and withdraw the announcement' is to talk sheer flapdoodle. I did not undertake to rewrite and bother myself with that infernal book for my own sweet pleasure. Could I annihilate it by hurling the accursed work into the 8th sphere I would. But my own predilections or wishes have naught to do with my duty. MASTER orders and wills it be rewritten and rewrite it I *will*; so much the better for those who will help me on the tedious task, and so·much *the worse for those who* do not and will not. Who knows but with God's blessing and help the thing may turn out 'a splendid piece of work' anyhow. Nor will I ever, with your permission and begging your pardon, of course, agree with you that 'it is madness to try and write such a book for monthly parts' *once that the Guru so ordains it*. For, notwithstanding the remarkable respect I feel for your Western wisdom and business-like talents, I would never say of anything my Master (in particular) and *the* Masters (in general) tell me to do—that it is sheer madness to do their bidding. One chapter at any rate, 'on the Gods and Pitris, the Devas and the Daïmonia, Elementaries and Elementals, and other like spooks' is finished. I have found and followed a very easy method given me, and chapter after chapter and part

---

[7] *The Word*, Vol. XV, April 1912, pp. 19 and 21.

[8] *The Letters of H.P. Blavatsky to A.P. Sinnett*, London and New York, 1924, p. 64.

after part will be rewritten very easily. Your suggestion that it must not 'look like a mere reprint of Isis' is nowhere in the face of the announcement (which please see in *The Theosophist* last page). Since it promises only 'to bring the matter contained in Isis' within the reach of all; and to explain and show that the 'later revelations' i.e., *Esot. Buddhism*, for one, and other things in *The Theosophist* are not contradictory to the outlines of the doctrine given—however *hazy* the latter is in that *Isis*; and to give in the *Secret Doctrine* all that is *important* in 'Isis' grouping together the materials relating to any given subject instead of leaving them scattered throughout the 2 vol. as they are now—then it follows that I am bound to give *whole pages* from 'Isis' only amplifying and giving additional information. And unless I do give numerous reprints from *Isis*, it will become *Osiris* or *Horus*—never what it was originally promised in the 'Publisher's Notice' which—please read.

And now having opened one of the safety-valves in my steam engine—I beg to subscribe myself ever your friend and well- wisher.

WIDOW BLAVATSKY.[9]

Sometime in the summer of 1884, in a letter received by A.P. Sinnett from Master K.H., the statement was made that:

The Secret Doctrine will explain many things, set to right more than one perplexed student.[10]

As the year of 1885 opened, Col. Olcott made the following remark in his *Diaries:*

H.P.B. gets from [M].[11] the plan for her 'Secret Doctrine' and it is excellent. Oakley and I had tried our hands at it last night, but this is much better.

H.P.B. who had come back to Adyar at the end of 1884, left it again for Europe on 31 March 1885, accompanied by Miss Mary Flynn, Bawaji (Dharbagiri Nāth), and Dr Franz Hartmann. Writing to Col. Olcott on 11 April 1885, while on board the *SS. Pei Ho*, nearing Aden, she said:

It appears that (1) Hartmann is determined to get the *Secret Doctrine* from me and have it printed in America (I wish he may get it); (2) he is as determined to persuade me to go with him to America (!!!). I believe the man must be crazy. Now listen. When preparing to go on the steamer, Subba Row told me to write the Secret Doctrine and send to him through you every week what I had written. I promised this to him and will do so. Now you must, to avoid useless quarrels with H., facilitate in the task. In your first letter write to me to remind me of this. Say that I must do as I

---

[9] *Letters to Sinnett*, Letter No. XXXVI, pp. 88-89.

[10] *Mahatma Letters*, Letter No. LXIII, p. 357; 3rd rev. ed., p. 351.

[11] His cryptogram only, in the *Diary*.

promised to Subba Row—send to him weekly what I had written, as he is going to make notes and commentaries and then the T.S. will publish it.[12]

Dr F. Hartmann, writing to Mrs Charles Johnston, from Hallein, 2 June 1893, noted the following fact:

> ... in April, 1885, when I accompanied H.P. Blavatsky from Madras to Europe, while on board of the SS.*Tibre* and on the open sea, she very frequently received in some occult manner many pages of manuscript referring to *The Secret Doctrine*, the material of which she was collecting at the time. Miss Mary Flynn was with us, and knows more about it than I.[13]

Having settled in Würzburg, Germany, in August 1885, still greatly disturbed over the Coulomb affair, H.P.B. wrote to A.P. Sinnett saying:

> (3) I cannot *bind* myself to a promise of working *only* on the S.D.—or working on it at all to its end.[14]

When the Sinnetts visited her there in September of the same year,

> The 'Secret Doctrine' was still untouched. ... when my wife and I saw her in Germany ... some premonitory symptoms indicated that the preparation of the 'Secret Doctrine' might shortly be set on foot.[15]

It is likely that Sinnett meant here the resumption of steady work by H.P.B. on her manuscripts.

In an undated letter to Sinnett, written most likely in the early autumn of 1885, H.P.B. stated:

> But Master said to me that if 'nothing happened out of the way' (?) He would help and the Mahatma also, as they are often here now for the Secret Doctrine.[16]

As far as we know, 'Master' meant H.P.B.'s direct superior, Master Morya, and 'Mahatma' was the term she used for Master Koot Hoomi.

In late autumn, namely on 28 October 1885, H.P.B. writing to Col. Olcott, conveyed the idea that work was now under way in a more serious manner. She wrote:

> I have not much time now with the *Secret Doctrine*. I am only at the middle of Part I, but shall in a month or two send you the first six sections. I take from *Isis* only facts, leaving out everything in the shape of dissertations, attacks on Christianity

---

[12]. Transcribed from the original in the Adyar Archives.

[13] Wachtmeister, *Reminiscences*, etc., p. 109.   [14] *Letters to Sinnett*, Letter No. LV, p. 133.

[15] A.P. Sinnett, *Incidents*, etc., 1886, pp. 302-03.   [16] *Letters to Sinnett*, Letter CXIX, p. 253.

and Science—in short, all the useless stuff, and all that has lost its interest. Only myths, symbols, and dogmas explained from an *esoteric* point of view. It is actually and *de facto* a new work entirely. Cycles are explained, along with everything else, from their occult bearings. I wish you had sent me the Preface, or Introduction.[17]

After H.P.B. had worked for some time in relative loneliness at Würzburg, Countess Constance Wachtmeister was 'sent' to help her, arriving there in the early part of December. To quote her own words:

> At this time I learned little more concerning *The Secret Doctrine* than that it was to be a work far more voluminous than *Isis Unveiled*, that it would consist when complete of four volumes, and that it would give out to the world as much of the esoteric doctrine as was possible at the present stage of human evolution. 'It will, of course, be very fragmentary,' she [H.P.B.] said, 'and there will of necessity be great gaps left, but it will make men think, and as soon as they are ready more will be given out. But,' she added after a pause, 'that will not be until the next century, when men will begin to understand and discuss this book intelligently.'
>
> Soon, however, I was entrusted with the task of making fair copies of H.P.B.'s manuscript, and then of course I began to get glimpses of the subject matter of *The Secret Doctrine*.[18]

She describes also how deeply H.P.B. was wounded by the false report of the Society for Psychical Research, and how it affected her work, compelling her at times to write out twelve times a page that she could not manage to write down correctly because of her disturbed state of mind.

The Countess relates that the circumstance which most attracted her attention and excited her wonder was 'the poverty of her travelling library'. Yet, 'her manuscripts were full to overflowing with references, quotations, allusions, from a mass of rare and recondite works on subjects of the most varied kind'.

By comparison with the writing of *Isis Unveiled*, as to quotations used and references made throughout her manuscripts, it seems that H.P.B. may have exercised her clairvoyant powers to a larger extent in writing *The Secret Doctrine*. The circumstances under which much of it was written, the geographical location in which she was (at least as far as her stay at Würzburg is concerned), and the absence of close friends and associates, warrant this deduction. On this subject, we have further testimony from the Countess who also quotes Miss Emily Kislingbury. She writes.

---

[17] Excerpt quoted by Col. Olcott in his *Old Diary Leaves*, Series III, p. 317. The original of this letter is unavailable.

[18] Wachtmeister, *op. cit.* pp. 23-24.

If ever H.P.B. wanted definite information on any subject which came uppermost in her writing, that information was sure to reach her in one way or another, either in a communication from a friend at a distance, in a newspaper or a magazine, or in the course of our casual reading of books; and this happened with a frequency and appositeness that took it quite out of the region of mere coincidence. She would, however, use normal means in preference to the abnormal when possible, so as not to exhaust her power unnecessarily.

I was not alone in remarking the assistance that came unsought to H.P.B. in the prosecution of her task, and the accuracy of the quotations that she received, and I insert here a note sent me by Miss E. Kislingbury, which illustrates the point and sets it in a strong light.

'After the publication of the now famous Psychical Society's Report, of which I felt strongly the injustice, I determined to go and see Madame Blavatsky, then living, I was told, at Würzburg. I found her living quietly in the quaint old German town, with the Countess Wachtmeister, who had stayed with her all the winter. She was ill, suffering from a complication of disorders, and under constant medical treatment. She was harassed, mentally, by the defection of friends and the petty assaults of enemies, in consequence of the above-named Report, and yet, in face of all these difficulties, H.P.B. was engaged on the colossal task of writing *The Secret Doctrine*. In a foreign town, the language of whose inhabitants was unfamiliar to her, with only such books as she had carried with her from India, far from any friends who could have helped her in finding needful references or making useful notes, she toiled away, rarely leaving her desk, except for meals, from early morning till six o'clock in the evening. But H.P.B. had her invisible helpers as she sat writing in the room sacred to her work. As I was not at that time a member of the T.S., though I had known H.P.B. almost since its foundation, little was said either *to* me or *before* me of the methods used. One day, however, she brought me a paper with a quotation which had been given her from some Catholic writer on the relation between science and religion, and asked whether I could help her in verifying it, as to the author and work in which it occurred. It struck me, from the nature of the quotation, that it might be from Cardinal Wiseman's *Lectures on Science and Religion*, and I wrote to a friend in London, with the result that the verification was complete, chapter and page being found, as it now stands in *The Secret Doctrine*, Vol. II, p. 704.'[19]

Writing to A.P. Sinnett some time in November 1885, H.P.B. said:

I am very busy on *Secret D.* The thing at N.Y. is repeated—only far clearer and better. I begin to think it *shall vindicate* us. Such pictures, panoramas, scenes *antediluvian* dramas with all that! Never saw or heard better...[20]

Writing to Col. Olcott under date of 25 November 1885, H.P.B. said:

[19] Wachtmeister, *Reminiscences*, pp. 36-37.
[20] *Letters to Sinnett*, Letter No. CXVI, p. 244.

Ah, you think I cannot write the S.D. without *you* or anyone sitting near me and helping? Well you shall soon find out your mistake. I have three Chap. ready, the *fourth* nearly finished and the S.D. shall be another, quite another kind of a hair-pin than *Isis*. It is a song from quite another opera, dear. Say the word or rather Subba Row and if he is willing to be looking over the MSS and correct them or add, or take out—then *I am willing by return post* to send what I have to Adyar. But you shall have to go over the *Introduction*. Sinnett can never be a 'chandelier' nor do I want any one. He is all the time offering and I consent only for the sake of the more elegant English and good ideas for mechanical arrangement, literary not metaphysical.

Well say the word—by return post and I shall send what I have ready. But you must be very careful that there should be no repetitions in such case as I shall have no MS. to refer to.[21]

H.P.B.'s progress with her work is confirmed by Dr William Hübbe-Schleiden who wrote saying:

When I visited her in October, 1885, she had just begun to write it, and in January 1886, she had finished about a dozen chapters.[22]

In a letter written from Würzburg to Dr Franz Hartmann, probably in December 1885, H.P.B. speaks rather enthusiastically about her writing. She says:

Now, as you know, I also am occupied with my book. It took possession of me (the epidemic of writing) and crept on 'with the silent influence of the itch', as Olcott elegantly expresses it—until it reached the fingers of my right hand, got possession of my brain—carried me completely into the region of the occult. I have written in a fortnight more than 200 pages (of the *Isis* shape and size). I write day and night, and now feel sure that my *Secret Doctrine* shall be finished this—no, not *this*—year, but the next. I have refused your help, I have refused Sinnett's help and that of everyone else, I did not feel like writing—now I do. I am permitted to give out for each chapter a page out of the Book of Dzyan—the oldest document in the world, of that I am sure—and to comment upon and explain its symbology. I think really it shall be worth something, and hardly here and there a few lines of dry facts from *Isis*. It is a completely new work.[23]

On 25 December 1885, the Countess writes to A.P. Sinnett and for the first time broaches the idea of actual publication, but speaks in terms of 'pamphlets' as the idea of serial publication must have still prevailed at the time. She says:

---

[21] Transcribed from the original in the Adyar Archives.

[22] Wachtmeister, *Reminiscences*, etc., p. 112.

[23] *The Path*, New York, Vol. X, January, 1896, pp. 299-300.

Madame would be very glad if Mr Sinnett would kindly begin to make enquiries about publication, etc., with prices, she would like the pamphlet to be about the size of *The Platonist*,[24] different from ordinary magazines—there will be two chapters each month, every chapter containing about 90 of her written sheets. She wishes the type to be a large and distinct one. Madame hopes shortly to send the Preface with 1st Chapter to Mr Sinnett.[25]

The year 1886 opens with a letter dated January 4 from the Countess to A.P. Sinnett who, apparently, had responded to the idea of publication and had made some sort of offer, the nature of which is not very clear. She says:

Madame is delighted with your proposition about the S.D. She thinks it is the most favourable and satisfactory arrangement for herself, but she says the journal must come out every month or if you think it better, every three months, for if she lives she believes so much will be given to her that it will last 3 years or more. The size of the Journal you can arrange as you think best. There will be no regular preface, only about 6 or 7 pages addressed to the Readers to give them an idea of what the book will contain, for otherwise they would be plunging wholesale into matter entirely unknown to them. Madame will send you shortly the Title pages, and in a week or so the address to the Reader with first two chapters. From this you will be able to judge of the general purpose of the whole work.[26]

It is to the early part of 1886, most likely January, that belong the famous 'certificates' on the subject of *The Secret Doctrine* received by Dr William Hübbe-Schleiden from Masters M. and K.H. The circumstances connected with this fact are of very special interest and deserve most careful consideration.

Dr William Hübbe-Schleiden was a German scholar, greatly interested in geographical exploration and in German colonial politics. He was born at Hamburg, 20 October 1846, and died at Göttingen, 17 May 1916. At first, he studied jurisprudence and political economy, obtaining the degree of *juris utriusque doctor,* i.e., Doctor of both Laws, namely, civil and canon law, and practised for some time as an attorney. During the war of 1870-71, he was attaché to the German Consulate General in London. Soon after, he devoted himself to far-reaching travel, mainly in West Africa, where he founded his·

---

[24] A metaphysical and occult monthly journal edited by Thos. M. Johnson, first at St Louis, Mo., then at Orange, N.Y., and later at Osceola, Mo. Its four volumes cover the period from February 1881 to June 1881, with a few breaks in between. It was superseded by *Bibliotheca Platonica.* Its files have become very scarce.

[25] *Letters to Sinnett,* Letter No. CXXIII, p. 268.

[26] *Letters to Sinnett,* Letter No. CXXVII, p. 271.

own commercial house in the Gabon Colony. He was a great protagonist of German colonial ambitions, and wrote several works on this subject, such as: *Ethiopien: Studien über Westafrika* (1879), *Überseeische Politik* (2 pts., 1881-83). *Deutsche Kolonisation* (1881), and *Kolonisationpolitik* und *Kolonisationtechnik* (1882). During the years 1897-98 he travelled in India, and upon his return wrote a work entitled *Indien und die Inder* (1898). There is evidence to show that he was instrumental in formulating German colonial policy at the time, and that his scheme was adopted by Prince Bismarck.

As a man, Dr Hübbe-Schleiden was a charming personality, full of humour, very clever, and always ready to help others. He was greatly interested in occultism, and became one of the chief founders and the first President of the Germania Theosophical Society when the latter was organized by Col. H.S. Olcott at the home of the Gebhards at Elberfeld, on 27 July 1884. His theosophical activities primarily took a literary form, and he founded and edited a monthly metaphysical journal called the *Sphinx*, twenty-two volumes of which appeared between the years 1886-96. Some years later, after Dr Rudolf Steiner organized a society of his own, Dr Hübbe-Schleiden served for a short time as General Secretary of the re-organized Theosophical Society in Germany.

Dr Hübbe-Schleiden considered *The Secret Doctrine* to be a work of utmost importance, actually containing the sacred wisdom of the sages of all times. He had found in its pages the keys which could 'solve the riddles of existence as well of *macrocosm* as of the *microcosm*'. He felt strongly that explanatory abstracts should be written on various teachings contained in this work in order that the contents might be better understood by readers of his time. It was with this end in view that in 1891 he wrote his work entitled *Lust, Leid und Liebe*, which, in his own words, 'confined itself to the language and to the terms of Darwin, Haeckel and modern philosophy, with the purpose of putting a key to *The Secret Doctrine* into the hands of the leading scientists'. His effort found no response with the English public, and only a meagre one in Germany.

Dr Hübbe-Schleiden dedicated his last years to a large work on Palingenesis, in which he desired to prove scientifically the law of rein-carnation. He died, however, before completing this task. After his death, his books were donated to the Göttingen University Library, and it is possible that the voluminous manuscript of this last work may have been there for a time. It was either destroyed during the bombing of the Second World War, or was otherwise lost, because, upon inquiry, it could not be located by the university authorities.

Dr Hübbe-Schleiden knew H.P.B. personally and paid her four or five visits of indefinite duration. The first of these was from September to December 1884, when she was staying with the Gebhards at Elberfeld. He speaks of meeting her for a few days in August of the same year. After that, he remained with her in Würzburg for about a week or ten days in October 1885, and saw her engaged in writing her *magnum opus*. He saw her last one afternoon and night, early in January 1886. He writes:

> When I visited her in October 1885, she had just begun to write it [*The Secret Doctrine*], and in January 1886, she had finished about a dozen chapters ... she was writing at her manuscript almost all day, from the early morning until the afternoon and even until night, unless she had guests... I also saw her write down sentences as if she were copying them from something before her, where, however, I saw nothing. I did not pay much attention to the manner of her work from the standpoint of a hunter of phenomena, and did not control it for that purpose; but I know that I saw a good deal of the well-known blue K.H. handwriting as corrections and annotations on her manuscripts as well as in books that lay occasionally on her desk. And I noticed this principally in the morning before she had commenced her work. I slept on the couch in her study after she had withdrawn for the night, and the couch stood only a few feet from her desk. I remember well my astonishment one morning when I got up to find a great many pages of foolscap covered with that blue pencil handwriting lying on her own manuscript, at her place on her desk. How these pages got there I do not know, but I did not see them before I went to sleep and no person had been bodily in the room during the night, for I am a light sleeper.
>
> I must say though that the view I took then was the same that I hold now. I never did and never shall judge of the value or the origin of any mental product from the way and manner in which it is produced. And for this reason I withheld my opinion then, thinking and saying: 'I shall wait until *The Secret Doctrine* is finished and then I can read it quietly; that will be the test for me, the only one that will be any good.'
>
> This is the reason *why* on the night of my last parting from H.P.B., the two *certificates* ... were given to me. At least I found them in my copy of Hodgson's S.P.R. Report after I had left her.[27]

Besides the two certificates spoken of by Dr Hüubbe- Schleiden, two more letters dealing with other subjects were received by him from the same Teachers. The original letters became part of his estate in 1916, and passed into the hands of Herr Clemens Heinrich Ferdinand Driessen, who was a Geheim

---

[27] From a letter received by Countess Constance Wachtmeister from Dr Wm. Hübbe-Schleiden sometime in 1893. See *Reminiscences of H.P. Blavatsky and 'The Secret Doctrine,'* by C. Wachtmeister (London: Theosophical Publishing Society, 1893) pp. 110-14.

Faithfully yours
Dr. Hubbe Schleiden

DR. WILLIAM
HÜBBE-SCHLEIDEN
1846-1916

COUNTESS CONSTANCE
WACHTMEISTER
1838-1910

COLONEL HENRY STEEL OLCOTT
1832-1907

Justitzrat in Witzenhausen, near Kassel. C. Jinarājadāsa copied them direct from the originals which had been loaned to him by Herr Driessen, and published their text in the *Letters from the Masters of the Wisdom.*[28] Ernst Pieper, a very active theosophical worker in Düsseldorf, obtained from Herr Driessen in 1934 all the four original letters with their accompanying envelopes, bearing on one side Chinese characters. He arranged for an exact facsimile to be made of the 'certificate' from Master M., reproducing it in its actual size of four-and-a-half by seven-two-eighths inches for the letter, and five by two and three-quarters inches for an envelope, and using an almost identical type of paper and red-coloured ink, so that the facsimile would be as perfect as possible. It is from this fascimile of Ernst Pieper that FIGURES I and I-A have been reproduced.

The text of this letter from Master M. is as follows:[29]

> If this can be of any use or help to Dr Hübbe- Schleiden,—though I doubt it—I, the humble undersigned Fakir, certify that the 'Secret Doctrine' is dictated to Upasika partly by myself & partly by my Brother K.H.
>
> M ∴.

Upāsikā means a female disciple, and stands for H.P.B.

The text of the second 'certificate' received by Dr Hübbe-Schleiden, written in blue crayon, and which, according to Ernst Pieper, was contained in a separate envelope similar to the first one, was as follows:[30]

> I wonder if this note of mine is worthy of occupying a select spot with the documents reproduced,[31] and which of the peculiarities of the 'Blavatskian' style of writing it will be found to most resemble? The present is simply to satisfy the Dr. that—'the more proof given the less believed'. Let him take my advice and not make these two documents public. It is for his own satisfaction that the undersigned is happy to assure him that *The Secret Doctrine* when ready, will be the triple production of M . . , Upasika and the Doctor's most humble servant.
>
> S.E.C.[32]   K.H.

In 1941, all the four original letters from the Teachers, received by Dr Hübbe-Schleiden, fell into the hands of the Gestapo and were presumably destroyed.

---

[28] Second Series. Adyar: Theosophical Publishing House, 1925; Chicago: The Theosophical Press. 1926. Letters Nos. 68, 69, 70, 71.

[29] Op. cit., Letter No. 70   [30] *Op. cit.,* Letter No. 69

[31] In Richard Hodgson's Report, published by the Society for Psychical Research in its Proceedings, Vol. III, Part ix, December 1885.

[32] The meaning of these initials is unknown.

2

FIGURE I   FIGURE I-A

Facsimiles of letter from Master M. to Dr Hübbe-Schleiden and of the envelope in which it was enclosed. On one side of the envelope appeared the addressee's name, and on the other the Chinese characters which convey the message:

'May great good fortune be at your service.'

As far as is known, therefore, of the four letters received direct by Dr Hübbe-Schleiden only the one from Master M., on the subject of *The Secret Doctrine*, was ever produced in facsimile, together with its accompanying envelope.

It would appear, however, that at the time when Dr Hübbe-Schleiden received the two 'certificates' from the Masters, 'copies were given from the same source to others for use in the future', as is stated by William Quan Judge in *The Path* (New York), Vol. VIII, April 1893, p. 2, where he published the text of these copies.[33]

These copies, however, were very obviously not made by ordinary means. They were precipitations (or re-precipitations) themselves. According to Mr Judge's own entry in his *Diary*, made in London under date of 21 July 1892, H.P.B. sent him these copies.

The originals of the two 'certificates' which were re-precipitated for Judge's benefit are in the William Quan Judge file held in the Archives of The Theosophical Society, Pasadena, California, and were reproduced in facsimile in *The Theosophical Forum*, Vol. XXVI, April 1948.

The precipitated copy of the letter from Master M. made for Mr Judge, diagonally written in red crayon, is almost completely faded. FIGURE II is the best reproduction of it that can be made today. Upon inspection, it is interesting to note, however, that it is not absolutely identical with the facsimile which appears in FIGURE I. It does not vary from it as far as the text is concerned, but its arrangement line for line is different. Its faithful transcription would be thus:

If this/can be any/use or help to/Dr Hübbe-Schleiden/—though I doubt it—/I, the humble undersigned/Fakir, certify that the/Secret Doctrine is dictated/to Upasika partly by myself/and partly by my Brother/K.H.

M ∴

The copy of the letter from Master K.H. made for Mr Judge was precipitated in the usual blue crayon; it is very clear and is reproduced as FIGURE III. It will be noticed that it is actually addressed 'To Dr Hübbe-Schleiden' and is marked 'Copy'. In the second sentence, the ninth word 'that', and in the fourth sentence, the seventh word 'that', which were in the original letter to Dr Hübbe-Schleiden, are omitted. The title of the 'Secret Doctrine' is not underlined.

---

[33] The article by Mr Judge is entitled 'Authorship of *The Secret Doctrine*' and may also be found in *Echoes of the Orient*: The Writings of William Quan Judge. Compiled by Dara Eklund. Point Loma Publications, Inc., San Diego, Calif., 1975, See Volume I, pp. 321 *et seq.*

It should also be noted that Master M.'s diagonally written letter in red crayon has been precipitated on the back of the sheet which bears Master K.H.'s letter in blue crayon.

About a year later, certain doubts having arisen in the minds of some people, three other communications from the same Teachers were sent, precipitated in the usual blue and red crayons. FIGURES IV and IV-A are reproductions of the originals which are in the William Quan Judge file held in the Archives of The Theosophical Society, Pasadena, California. The text of the letter sent to W.Q. Judge from Master K.H. reads as follows:

> The certificates given last year saying that the Secret Doctrine would be when finished the triple production of Upasika, M ∴. and myself was and is correct, although some have doubted not only the facts given in it but also the authenticity of the message in which it was contained. Copy this and also keep the copy of the aforesaid certificate. You will find them both of use on the day when you shall, as will happen without your asking, receive from the hands of the very person to whom the certificate was given, the original for the purpose of allowing you to copy it; and then you can verify the correctness of this presently forwarded copy. And it may then be well to indicate to those wishing to know what portions in the Secret Doctrine have been copied by the pen of Upasika into its pages, though without quotation marks, from my own manuscript and perhaps from M ∴. though the last is more difficult from the rarity of his know[n] writing and greater ignorance of his style.[34] All this and more will be found necessary as time goes on but for which you are well qualified to wait.
>
> K.H.

Below the letter from K.H., the following was added:

> The Dr. will be in the same rut for many years. Go on and fear nothing. I am beside you when you least expect it. No, this is not my personal style—the latter in a language you could not read—Yes right, the whole age transits—Particulars not given.
>
> M ∴.

The prophecy contained in the first of these two letters, namely the one from Master K.H., came true in every particular. Dr Hübbe-Schleiden showed Mr Judge his own original letters from the Teachers. As stated by him: '*I am the person who showed them to Mr Judge in London last August.*[35] From the

---

[34] As far as is known, no such listing or tabulation of passages has ever been made.
[35] Rather 21 July 1892.

advice given me in the one signed K.H., I was not to publish them, but Mr Judge was authorized to do so by the instructions which *he* received.' [36] This is further confirmed by Mr Judge himself whose entry in his *Diary*, under date of 21 July 1892, reads: '... Hübbe-Schleiden arrives had conference. ... He lends me Masters letters to him. Same as copies sent me by H.P.B.'

At first, it may appear puzzling to the student to understand what Master K.H. meant when stating in the above letter that the correctness of the original certificates can be verified by 'this presently forwarded copy'. Seeing that such a copy was 'presently forwarded', this reference cannot stand for the copies received by Mr Judge about a year before. The puzzle is explained by the existence in the Judge file in the above mentioned archives of another communication, written in black pencil (except for the last line which is in red) and being an *almost* verbatim copy of the certificates received in January 1886. Curiously enough this entire communication is precipitated in the handwriting of Master M., including the portion signed by K. H. FIGURES V and V-A are a facsimile of this message,[37] and the text reads as follows:

> I wonder if this note of mine is worthy of occupying a select spot with the documents reproduced and which of the peculiarities of the 'Blavatskian' style of writing it will be found to most resemble. The present is simply to satisfy the Dr that 'the more proof given the less believed.'[38] — It is for his own satisfaction the undersigned is happy to assure him that the Secret Doctrine when ready will be the triple production of M . ., Upasika and the Doctor's —most humble servant.
>
> K.H.
>
> If this can be of any use or help to Dr Hübbe-Schleiden—though I doubt it——I the humble undersigned Fakir certify that the Secret Doctrine is dictated to Upasika partly by myself and partly by my brother K.H.
>
> M . .
>
> [*Underneath the diagonal line:*]
> Omitting signatures it might be used in the book
>
> M . .
>
> [*The last sentence, written in red crayon, reads:*]
> An effort to defend the teacher cannot fail [39]

---

[36] C. Wachtmeister, *op. cit.*, p. 113.

[37] Originally reproduced in The *Theosophical Forum*, Vol. XXVI, April 1948.

[38] The sentence: 'Let him take my advice and not make these two documents public', which appears in K.H.'s original certificate, as well as in the one marked 'copy', is not included here by Master M.   [39] This short sentence bears no signature.

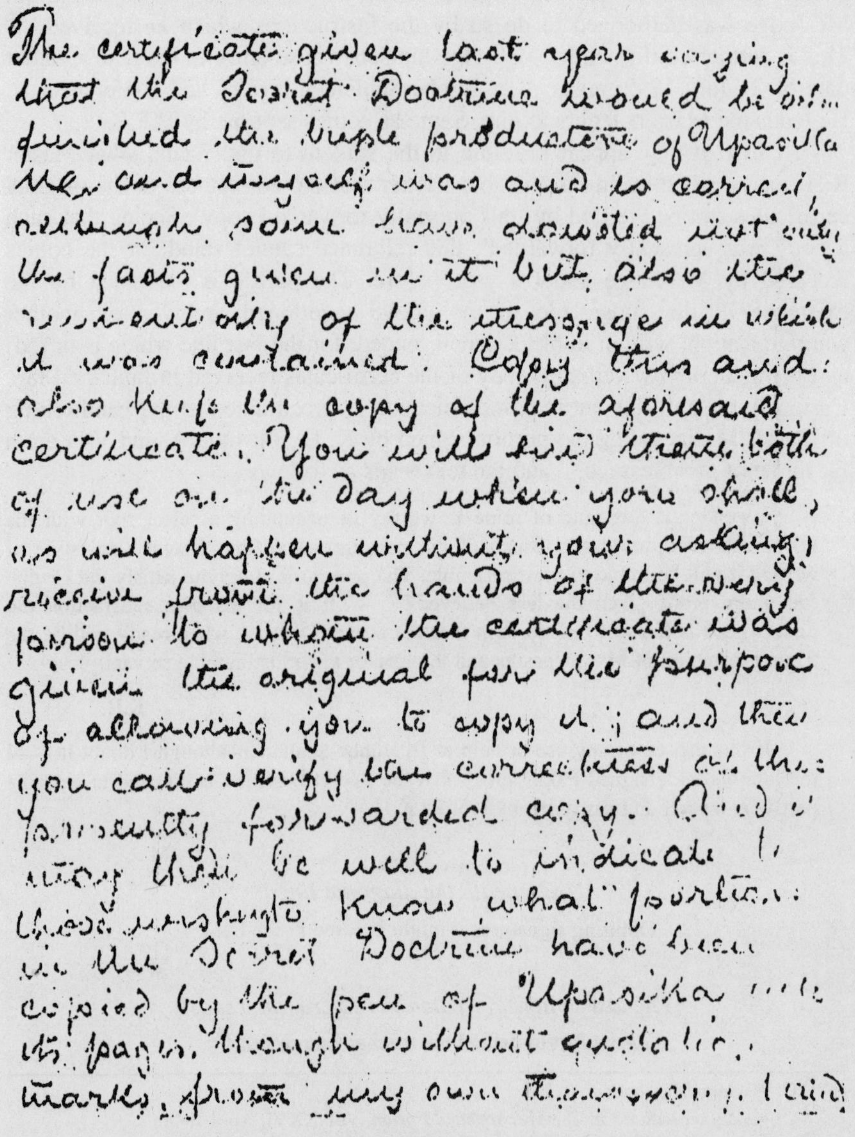

[Facsimile of handwritten letter]

FIGURE IV
Facsimile of letter from Master K.H. to William Quan Judge.
From the Archives of The Theosophical Society, Pasadena,
California. Reproduced with permission.

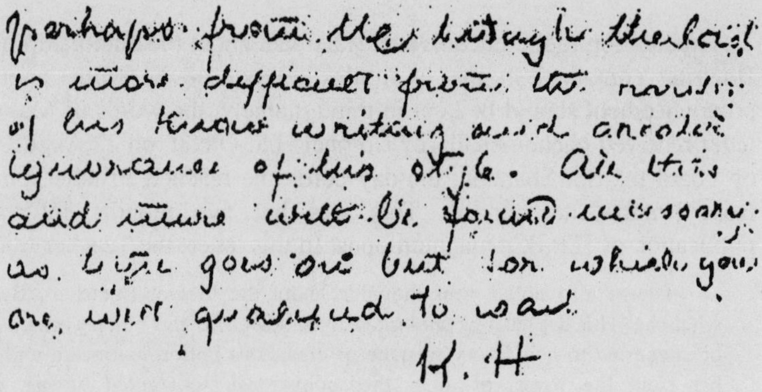

perhaps from the literary standpoint is more difficult from the novelty of his known writing and another ignorance of his style. All this and more will be found necessary as life goes on but for which you are well qualified to work.

K.H

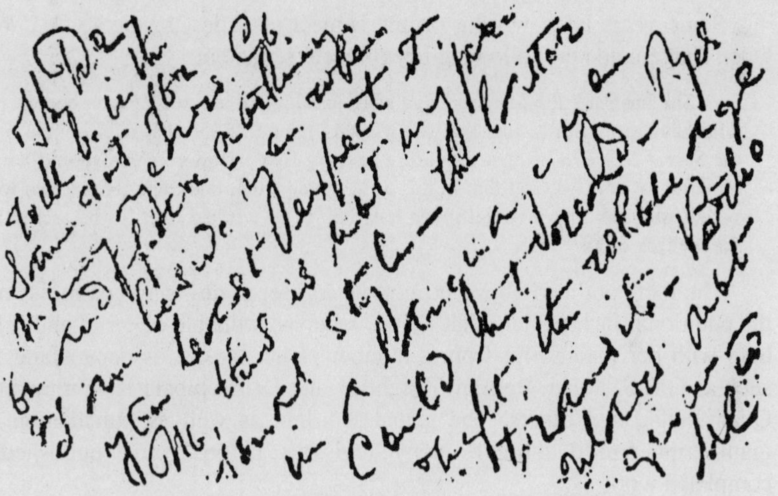

FIGURE IV-A

Facsimile of concluding portion of letter from Master K.H. and of the added message from Master M. to William Quan Judge.

From the Archives of The Theosophical Society, Pasadena, California. Reproduced with permission.

In addition to the unequivocal statement about the authorship of *The Secret Doctrine* contained in the facsimiles reproduced herewith, another definite pronouncement should be kept in mind, namely, the words of Master K.H. in a letter received phenomenally by Colonel H.S. Olcott, on 22 August 1888, while on board the SS. Shannon, the day before he reached Brindisi, on his journey from Bombay to London. This was but two months before the actual publication of H.P.B.'s magnum opus. In this letter, the Teacher said:

> I have also noted your thoughts about the 'Secret Doctrine'. Be assured that what she [H.P.B.] has not *annotated* from scientific and other works, we have given or *suggested* to her. Every mistake or erroneous notion, corrected and explained by her from the works of other theosophists *was corrected by me*, or *under my instruction*. It is a more valuable work than its predecessor, an epitome of occult truths that will make it a source of information and instruction for the earnest student for long years to come.[40]

Some years later, writing on the subject of 'The Closing Cycle', William Quan Judge made the following unequivocal statement:

> She has said, the Masters have said, and I again assert it for the benefit of those who have any faith in me, that the Masters have told me that they helped her write the *Secret Doctrine* so that the future seventy-five and more years should have some material to work on, and that in the coming years that book and its theories would be widely studied. The material given has then to be worked over, to be assimilated for the welfare of all.[41]

The facts outlined above do not, of course, in any way contradict or deny the additional fact, namely that H.P.B. received valuable editorial and scholarly help with her manuscript from a number of her closest associates and friends such as G.R.S. Mead, Bertram Keightley and Dr Archibald Keightley, William Quan Judge, and others. The actual wording as well as punctuation of her manuscript passed through many revisions before being published as a completed work.

From several sources, including H.P.B.'s letter to Col. Olcott dated 6 January 1886, it is apparent that the idea of making *The Secret Doctrine* a new version or revision of *Isis Unveiled* had by then been abandoned. The situation, as prevailing at the time, is shown by an excerpt from the above-mentioned letter:

---

[40] C. Jinarājadāsa, *Letters from the Masters of the Wisdom*. First Series. 4th ed., Adyar, Madras, 1948. Letter No. 19, p. 52.   [41] *The Irish Theosophist*, Vol. III, No. 4, January 1895.

I have the *Secret Doctrine* to show whether Masters are or *are not*. If not—then *I am* the Mahatma, and that's as well. See what Sinnett has arranged. A little better arrangement to begin with than *Isis* ever was. What you ought to do is to condense *Isis* throwing out all that is not to the point and letting it out in monthly parts (cheap) or in one Vol. better monthly, and sell it in India. For Secret Doctrine *is entirely* new. There will not be there 20 pages quoted by bits from *Isis*. New matter, occult explanations—the whole Hindu Pantheon explained based on exoteric translations (to be easily verified) and explained esoterically proving Xty and every other religion to have taken their dogmas from India's oldest religion. No word against any class, personalities *left out altogether*—missionaries entirely ignored, scientists except when quoted—*untouched*. In *four* Parts—Archaic, Ancient, Mediaeval and Modern Periods. Each Part 12 chapters, with Appendixes and a Glossary of terms at the end. Countess here, and she sees I have almost *no books*. Master and Kashmiri dictating in turn. She copies all. This *will be* my vindication, I tell you. *Preface* received from Adyar only came to be immediately *burnt* in the kitchen by myself and Countess. Thus you could easily, by sacrificing two copies of *Isis*, boil out of two Vol. 1 in parts and let it go for 8 or 10 rupees the whole 12 or 14 annas the number and keep money for Society. I could do it in a month had I time. Now listen. Secure the help of Subba [Row] for *Secret Doc*. Lots there of Adwaitism or *old* Aryan Religion occult which if *reinforced* by what S.R. can add will kill Hodgson and Co. on the spot. Shall he do it for you or rather for himself and Adwaitism? If he promises faithfully and you think he will do it I shall send you by two or three chapters at once; if not—I begin publishing here. Let him see first five or six chapt. and judge. We can take the public of India by storm if he helps me with old quotations and occult meanings added to mine. Answer at once. Because it will delay publication, unless you do. And I have to hurry on with my vindication. Now that I am here quite alone with no books around me and that S.D. will be twenty times as erudite as occult and explanatory people shall see I guess and judge.[42]

More or less the same is stated in her letter to Sinnett written the same date:

Now I am here alone with the Countess for witness. I have no books, no one to help me. And I tell you that the *Secret Doctrine* will be 20 times as learned, philosophical and better than *Isis* which will be killed by it.[43]

Fortunately, 'Isis' was neither killed nor even harmed, as its uninterrupted and rather rapid sales, edition after edition, have shown for almost a century.

Various interruptions often disturbed H.P.B.'s mind and reflected from time to time upon the progress of her work. We can easily gather this from the remarks of the Countess writing to Sinnett, 11 January 1886:

---

[42] Transcribed from the original in the Adyar Archives.
[43] *Mahatma Letters*, Letter No. CXL, p. 481; 3rd rev., ed. p. 473.

Not a word has been added to the S.D. since the 31st Dec., but if we can only get a few days of calm and quiet I hope Madame will be able to begin writing again.[44]

In a letter dated January 15 the Countess informs him that:

At last Madame has settled down again to the S.D., *a whole fortnight lost.*[45]

On January 28, however, the Countess tells him that:

The S.D. has again been put on one side, no work for a fortnight. Babajee's doing—it is too bad. I wonder what will come next.[46]

On February 1, she lets him know, however, that:

... She [H.P.B.] has settled down on the first day of the month to the S.D. All January *has been lost*, next to nothing done, first Selin, then Babajee.[47]

On January 19, Col. Olcott, writing to H.P.B., conveyed to her some new ideas and suggestions. He said:

You may send the MSS. in instalments: Subba Row will go over it with Oakley and it will be returned to you. He asked if he should be free to add or amend, to which I answered of course, it was for that he was requested to edit it. He then consented.

I have thought of a better plan than the others for publishing. Thick volumes like 'Isis' are too heavy to hold for reading and too expensive for poor people; the issue in monthly parts makes a constant nuisance of posting, collecting money, buying money orders, etc. There is also the risk of having a lot of broken sets left on your hands by many subscribers taking 2, 3, 4 or a half-dozen parts and then stopping, while we, counting on their continuing, print whole sets for them, and find ourselves with that number of odd parts that can't be sold and are only fit to use as packing for book parcels or to sell for old paper. My idea is to split the entire work into *four* volumes, each half as thick as a volume of 'Isis', to issue them (as Herbert Spencer does his works) seriatim, at what will be a moderate cost when paid for separately, and in the first volume to put a 'Table of Contents' showing what Vols. I, II, III and IV are to contain. This will induce the subscriber or buyer of Vol. I to buy all the others. To do this, you must have (*a*) a skeleton plot of the whole book; (*b*) the matter so arranged as to progressively lead the reader on to the end; (*c*) and no recurring to a topic after it is once passed; should you think of anything important later, it may be added in a Supplement, with references back in each case to the vol. and pp. when the subject was discussed. In short to do very opposite of

---

[44] *Letters to Sinnett*, Letter No. CXXVIII, p. 273.   [45] Ibid., Letter CXXIX, p. 273.
[46] Ibid., Letter CXXXVI, p. 282.   [47] Ibid., Letter No. CXXXVIII, pp. 283-84.

what we did in 'Isis', which was a sort of literary rag-bag, with contents higgledy-piggledy.[48]

In a letter written to Sinnett at about this time, H.P.B. says:

I will send to you two or three chapters of S.D. before I send them to Subba Row to India. I want you to see and read it for yourself before it passed through the hands of S.R., lest a Hodgson would say again that the S.D. was written by Subba Row as *Isis* presumably was. What I want now is WITNESSES.[49]

On February 16, in another letter to him, H.P.B., deeply hurt by various attacks and misrepresentations from her own co-workers, expresses her feeling that there must be

... some means to be provided that I could finish or rather work on, until I finish the *Secret Doctrine*. Now in my present state it is *thoroughly impossible*.[50]

In February, Mr and Mrs Sinnett went to visit H.P.B. in Würzburg, staying there for about three weeks. H.P.B.'s aunt, Madame Nadyezhda A. de Fadeyev, and 'the Soloviovs' were there at approximately the same time. Sinnett went over dates, etc., for his *Incidents*, and they agreed on the title of this forth-coming book. Apparently Sinnett left first, while his wife stayed longer. In a letter written to Col. Olcott during this period, the original of which no longer is available, H.P.B. says:

Sinnett has left, after stopping with me three weeks, and Mrs [S.] remains for ten days more. She is very kind, and copies for me the *Secret Doctrine*. The enormous (volume) of Introductory Stanzas, the first chapter on the Archaic Period and Cosmogony, with numberless appendices, is ready; but how to send it to Adyar? Suppose it is lost! I do not remember one word of it.[51]

On 3 March 1886, H.P.B., writing to Sinnett, appears to be again in 'high gear', as it were, and we learn a number of interesting facts. She says:

There's a new development and scenery, every morning. I live two lives again. Master finds that it is too difficult for me to be looking consciously into the astral light for my S.D. and so, it is now about a fortnight, I am made to see all I have to as though in my dream. I see large and long rolls of paper on which things are written and I recollect them. Thus all the Patriarchs from Adam to Noah were given me to see—parallel with the Rishis; and in the middle between them, the meaning of their

---

[48] *Letters to Sinnett*, Letter No. CLXVII, p. 326.   [49] Ibid., Letter No. LXXXIII, pp. 197.
[50] Ibid., Letter LXXVII, p. 182.   [51] H.S. Olcott, *Old Diary Leaves*, Series III, p. 366.

symbols—or personifications. Seth standing with Bhrigu for first *sub*-race of the root race, for inst.: meaning, *anthropologically*—first *speaking* human sub-race of the 3rd Race; and *astronomically*—(his years 912 y.) meaning at one and same time the length of the solar year in that period, the duration of his race and many other things—(too complicated to tell you now). Enoch finally, meaning the solar year when our present duration was settled, 365 days—('God took him when he was 365 years old') and so on. It *is* very complicated but I hope to explain it sufficiently clear. I have finished an enormous Introductory Chapter, or *Preamble*, Prologue, call it what you will; just to show the reader that the text as it goes, every Section beginning with a page of translation from the Book of *Dzyan* and the Secret Book of 'Maitreya Buddha' *Champai chhos Nga* (in prose, not the five books in verse known, which are a blind) are no fiction. I was ordered to do so, to make a rapid sketch of what *was* known historically and in literature, in classics and in profane and sacred histories—during the 500 years that preceded the Christian period and the 500 y. that followed it, of *magic*, the existence of a Universal Secret Doctrine known to the philosophers and Initiates of every country and even to several of the Church fathers such as Clement of Alexandria, Origen, and others, who had been initiated themselves. Also to describe the Mysteries and some rites; and I can assure you that most extraordinary things are given out now, the whole story of the Crucifixion etc., being shown to be based on a rite as old as the world—the Crucifixion on the *Lath* of the Candidate—trials, going down to Hell, etc., all Aryan. The whole story hitherto unnoticed by Orientalists is found even exoterically, in the *Puranas* and *Brahmanas*, and then explained and supplemented with what the *Esoteric* explanations give. How the Orientalists have failed to notice it passes comprehension. Mr Sinnett, dear, I have *facts* for 20 Vol. like *Isis*; it is the language, the cleverness for compiling them, that I lack. Well you will soon [see] this Prologue, the *short* survey of the forthcoming Mysteries in the text—which covers 300 pages of foolscap.[52]

Writing to Sinnett on March 12, the Countess tells him:

In reading the first chapter I got so confused over the 'Stanzas' and the 'Commentaries' that I could make nothing of them. Madame then wrote the former in *red ink*, the latter in *black ink*, and now they are far easier to comprehend as confusion of ideas is avoided; this has suggested the following idea, that in the S.D. the Stanza should be printed red and all foreign words of a separate colour, Tibetan yellow, Chinese blue, Greek violet, and so on. It would be original, and prevent confusion.[53]

---

[52] *Letters to Sinnett*, Letter, No. LXXX, pp. 194-95. See further where the subject of Volume III is discussed, and where this letter of H.P.B.'s is carefully analysed in its bearing upon a possible Volume III.

[53] *Letters to Sinnett*, Letter No. CXLVII, p. 294.

Without the slightest doubt, these were ideas and suggestions emanating from people who did not have the faintest idea either about methods of ordinary printing or about difficulties connected with colour-printing. Expenses connected with any such scheme would have been astronomical.

In a letter written from New York on March 22, William Quan Judge tells H.P.B. that:

> Your Secret Doctrine ought to be proteced here. As you are an American citizen that can be done. *Have Sinnett attend to that from his side*. If you do not he may neglect it.[54]

While H.P.B. herself, writing to Judge but two days later, (March 24) says:

> I want you badly for the arrangement of *Secret Doctrine*. Such facts, *such facts*, Judge, as Masters are giving out will rejoice your old heart.[55]

In April 1886, W.Q. Judge launched in New York *The Path* magazine, and its first issue carried the following Announcement:

> *The Secret Doctrine*—Madame H.P. Blavatsky is now engaged upon this work, in Germany, where she went last year for her health. The subject is interesting, and the result of the author's endeavors will mark an era. It will not only be an amplification and explanation of *Isis Unveiled*, but will contain mines of further information. There will be in it verbatim passages from the Book of Dzyan and Limri [Lamrim] of Tsong-Kha-pa, and old commentaries, to which, hitherto, access has not been possible, and great attention will be paid to the doctrine of Human Evolution, to Divine or White Magic, and Human or Black Magic. The portion in which the subject of the Divine Hermaphrodite is considered, should be of absorbing interest. It will be divided in four parts: Archaic, Ancient, Mediaeval and Modern, presenting the complete sequences of the development of Occultism and Magic in their religious and anti-religious aspects.[56]

In the spring of 1886, H.P.B. decided to move to Ostend. After visits from Dr F. Hartmann and Mary and Gustav Gebhard during the month of April, she left Würzburg on May 10 in company with Miss E. Kislingbury who had also come on a brief visit. Countess Wachtmeister saw her off and then left herself, together with Mrs Mary Gebhard, to visit Dr Hartmann and Kempten in Austria. On her way, via Cologne, H.P.B. was persuaded by Gustav Gebhard to break her journey at their hospitable home in Elberfeld. While there, she

---

[54] *Ibid.*, Letter No. CLX, p. 314. The sentence which appears in italics has been underlined by H.P.B. on the original of Mr Judge's letter.

[55] Wachtmeister, *Reminiscences*, etc., p. 101.

[56] *The Path*, New York, Vol. I, No. 1, April 1886, p. 29.

slipped on the parquet floor of her bedroom, and sprained her ankle and hurt her leg. She required a fairly long convalescence, during which her sister, Vera Petrovna de Zhelihovsky, and her niece, Vera Vladimirovna, came from Russia to visit her.

We have excerpts from two letters written by H.P.B. to the Countess from Elberfeld. In one of them she complains of the fact that

> The current of the *S.D.* has stopped, and it will take two months before I can regain that state in which I was at Würzburg.[57]

while in the other she makes a rather cryptic remark to the effect that:

> Manuscript to *The Secret Doctrine* comes back from our Revd. friend; he finds it far superior to the introductory—but not even half-a-dozen words corrected. He says it is *perfect.*[58]

There is no indication who the 'Revd. friend' may have been.

So far as we know, it was on July 8 that H.P.B., accompanied by her relatives, left Elberfeld for Ostend, via Brussels. It is possible that she stopped in Paris for a very short time, and, having reached her destination, settled at Villa Nova, 10 Boulevard Van Isgham.

Some time during the first or second week of July, H.P.B. wrote to the Countess saying:

> I am trying to write *The Secret Doctrine*. But Sinnett, who is here for a few days, wants all my attention directed to the blessed *Memoirs*. Mrs Sinnett was unable to come, and he will soon leave me.[59]

A letter written by H.P.B. to Col. Olcott, and dated 14 July 1886, explains many things. She writes:

> Well, about the *S.D.* How can I answer you what you ask? I asked Sinnett to do so, for it is to him to say when he has read what is now written. I will write about the arrangement in a mail or two. Of course S[ubba] R[ow]'s advice will be priceless and if you can make him keep the MSS. no longer than a month it will be excellent. But suppose he keeps it an indefinite time? It must be in parts,—says Sinnett, to go on as long as there will be a demand for it—indefinitely, and must be begun this fall. It will be so arranged that people will pay beforehand for that only which is already in the hands of the publisher, and must come out simultaneously here and in America—for which Redway is corresponding with Bouton. Now I will send to *your care* and on *your* responsibility the '*Preface* to the Reader' and the 1st chapter of the

---

[57] Wachtmeister, *Reminiscences*, etc., p. 41.
[58] Ibid., p. 62.   [59] Ibid., *Reminiscences*, etc., p. 63.

Secret Doctrine proper. There are 600 pages and more of foolscap as an Introductory Preliminary Book, showing the undeniable historically proven facts of the existence of Adepts before and after the Christian period, of the admission of a double esoteric meaning in the two Testaments by Church Fathers, and *proofs* that the real source of every Christian dogma rests in the Aryan oldest MYSTERIES during the Vedic and Brahmanic period, proofs and evidence for it being shown in the *Exoteric* as well as Esoteric Sanskrit works. This I will send after, if Subba Row approves of Chap. I which consists of *Seven Stanzas* taken from the Book of *Dzan* (or *Dzyan*) and is commented and glossed upon, as in the three glossaries upon it—in Sanskrit, Chinese, and Tibetan. I cannot part with it without having a copy, for, if lost on the way, or otherwise mutilated, I cannot rewrite it. Now I am *alone*; no one to copy or help me. In a fortnight I will send you the Preface and 1st Chapter. But you *must* force S.R. to read and not to put it by aside, leaving it at his leisure and pleasure as he always does.[60]

In connection with this period, however, we are running into some chronological uncertainties which are very difficult to clarify.

We have an unequivocal statement by the Countess to the effect that:

Just before leaving Würzburg, H.P.B. had sent her manuscripts for *The Secret Doctrine* to Adyar to Col. H.S. Olcott, the President of the Society. She was anxious to have his opinion as he had helped her so much with *Isis*. She also wished the manuscript to be submitted to Mr Subba Row, and few pages which he had read interested him so much that he was anxious to see more.[61]

The Countess describes how H.P.B. left Würzburg, and speaks of 'the serious task of piling up all the baggage, consisting of pillows, coverlets, handbags, and the precious box containing the manuscript of *The Secret Doctrine*; this was never to be out of her sight'.

The Countess returned to Sweden in July 1886, and in the autumn was back with H.P.B., this time at Ostend. H.P.B. apparently asked her to go to London to attend to some private business for her, and she quotes from a couple of letters she received from H.P.B. while there. The following excerpt is from one of them:

I sent a telegram yesterday asking whether I could send you to London my MSS., as I have to forward it without delay to Madras. It is all splendidly packed up by Louise's husband, corded and sewn in oil cloth, all secure for the journey, so you will have no trouble with it, but to have it insured. Please do this yourself. You are the only one in whom I have absolute faith. Olcott writes that Subba Row is so anxious about the MSS. that he is enquiring daily when it comes, etc., and Master

---

[60] Transcribed from the original in the Adyar Archives.   [61] *Reminiscences*, etc., p. 66.

ordered him, it appears, to look it over. Please send it on by this mail and do insure it for no less than £150 or £200, for if lost—well good-bye!—so I send it to you today to your address and do answer immediately you receive it.[62]

It is not possible to ascertain, though it is quite probable, that two different portions of the famous Manuscript are being spoken of—one that had gone to Adyar from Würzburg, and another which was about to go there. It is even probable that there were as many as three separate mailings in which various portions of this manuscript went to Adyar.

The Countess gives us excerpts from two other letters she received from H.P.B. while in London on an errand. In one of them, H.P.B. says:

I hear the people who subscribed to *The Secret Doctrine* are getting impatient—cannot be helped. I, *you know*, work fourteen hours a day. The last MSS. sent to Adyar will not be back for three months, but then we can begin publishing. Subba Row is making valuable notes, so Olcott tells me.

In another, H.P.B. tells her that:

Last night, instead of going to bed I was made to write till 1 o'clock. The *triple Mystery* is given out—one I had thought they would never have given out—that of...[63]

After rejoining H.P.B. and settling down with her, the Countess states that:

Mr Z. soon left, and then we recommenced our usual routine of life, and the writing of *The Secret Doctrine* was carried on strenuously.[64]

It is probable that Z. stands for Mr Zorn who was organizing theosophical work at Odessa in Russia.

Writing to Dr Anna Bonus Kingsford under date of August 23, H.P.B. says:

I am hard at work now, for I am afraid not to be able to finish my 'Secret Doctrine' if I wait long. Whatever it may be as a literary production, people will learn in it more than one new things.[65]

In a letter written to Sinnett and dated September 21, H.P.B. says:

I have sent Vol. I of the S.D. to Adyar and am now on Vol.II—the *Archaic*.[66]

---

[62] Ibid., etc., p. 66.

[63] *Reminiscences*, etc., pp. 67 and 68. The final dots in the second excerpt are in the Countess' quoted passage.

[64] Ibid., pp. 68-69.   [65] E. Maitland, *Anna Kingsford*, Vol. II, pp. 251-52.

[66] *Letters to Sinnett*, Letter No. C, p. 222.

Dr. Archibald Keightley
1859-1930

Bertram Keightley
1860-1945

WILLIAM QUAN JUDGE
1851-1896

We learn a number of interesting facts from H.P.B.'s letter to Col. Olcott dated 23 September 1886, in which another portion of the manuscript appears in view. She writes:

> I send you the MSS. of *Secret Doctrine* through Mrs Gebhard who will insure the thing for 3 or 4,000 marks—she took them with her to Elberfeld whither she returned. Now I send only 1st volume of *Introduct.* Section, and in a fortnight will send the real pucka *S.D.*, *Archaic* Period, the 7 Stanzas, from Book of *Dzyan* commented upon. There are in the 1st *Introductory* Vol. *Seven Sections* or Chapt. § and 27 Appendices, several App. attached to every Section from 1 to 6, etc. Now all this will make either more or at any rate one volume and it is not the S.D. but a Preface to it. It is an absolutely necessary one, otherwise if they begin reading the Archaic Vol. the public would get crazy before reading from pages *too metaphysical*. Now, it is so arranged that the Appendices can either go as attached to the Sections or be taken out and placed in a *separate* Vol. or at the end of each; but you cannot put the App. from the Vol. or Preliminary Sections in Vol. II or Book I, the Archaic; I have been careful to mark every page of App. with title Number and to what Sect. or Chap. it belongs to. If you take out the App. then there will not [be] 300 pages printed in Int. Sections, but they will lose in interest. Do, however, as you please, but do not lose pages and do not allow the thing to be mutilated. If you or S. Row find anything too much, cross it out lightly; and if you want to add, write the addition on a page and pin it to the page you add to. Remember—this is my last *great work*, I could not rewrite it if lost to save my life or that of the Society, which is more.[67]

From the above, the deduction seems inevitable that whatever manuscripts had been sent to Adyar to this date, more of them were to be dispatched before long.

H.P.B.'s letter to Sinnett written sometime in the autumn of that year contains the following information:

> ... then he [Djual Khool] told me that Master sent in a word for you, and me to tell you; 'Sinnett has evidently forgotten what he had read in the Comm. on the 7 Stanzas (Book II Archaic period). Otherwise he would have known that out of what is plainly stated there, seven such pamphlets (as about *protyle*) could be written by Mr Crookes if he only knew it. No such scientific *orthodox* terms used in the S.D. but all that can be given out in *this* century is there and about chemistry and physics more than anything else. If Mr Sinnett is willing to read those portions to Mr Crookes—or Mr Crookes wants to read them himself—send the MSS. to them by all means...

---

[67] Transcribed from the original in the Adyar Archives

3

It is true that ever since you left, Master has made me add something daily to the old MSS. so that much of it *is* new and much more that I do not understand myself.[68]

On 18 October 1886, H.P.B., writing a rather pathetic letter to her staunch friend G. Subbiah Chetty at Adyar, said:

I am generally in poor health and my Secret Doctrine absorbs all my attention and takes up all my time.

and added in a P.S.:

Please tell Olcott that if as he thinks Subba Row has no time to go through the S.D. I better not send it to Adyar.[69]

The Theosophist for October 1886 (Vol. VIII, p. 62) has the following statement in an unsigned paragraph entitled 'Literary and Personal Notes', and which most likely was written by Col. Olcott:

It is gratifying to learn that the 'Secret Doctrine' is steadily growing. Mr Sinnett writes that as much as would make about one volume of 'Isis' is already written; and from another source we learn that, in its profundity of analysis and erudition, as well as in the arrangement of its matter, it will be superior to 'Isis'. Though the Manager long ago offered to return the money to the registered subscribers, scarcely any availed themselves of it, seeming to instinctively comprehend that books like these cannot be tossed off like an ephemeral novel, but are the work of years. The actual writing of 'Isis' occupied two years of uninterrupted labor, such labor that for six months at a time Madame Blavatsky never left her apartments, but sat writing constantly. Since she announced 'The Secret Doctrine' as in preparation, she has twice been confined to bed for weeks together, and once just escaped death by a miracle; besides having to endure the annoyance of the late conspiracy against her, which was hardly congenial to the book-writing frame of mind. However, the work grows apace, and no doubt the old proverb will be verified that 'Patient waiting is no loss'.

The attitude of T. Subba Row was becoming very unfavourable. He was rather moody at times, and his Brahmanical upbringing was influencing him to a considerable extent. He was against the disclosure of any higher esoteric teachings; his distrust of Occidentals was acute, and he never fully accepted the fact that occult teachings could be given out so freely by a 'woman'. These must have been peculiarities of his personal makeup, as he was in reality a high chela of Master M., H.P.B.'s own Teacher, and was unquestionably an Initiate

---

[68] *Letters to Sinnett*, Letter No. CIII, pp. 225-26.
[69] Transcribed from the original in the Adyar Archives.

of one or another degree. The collaboration of Subba Row in the production of
The Secret Doctrine was becoming more and more doubtful every day.

We have one more passage of H.P.B.'s in a letter to Sinnett written some
time during the same autumn. She says:

> Meanwhile I am *impressed* to send you a few pages that I have *unhooked* from
> my Book I, Archaic Period, the beginning of which you have seen and beg you to
> read them carefully. Now if you do not find in it your *prolix* or his—whatever its
> name—than I am a Battenberg! This was written at *Villa Nova* when you left and the
> Countess has copied it all long ago. Only for mercy's sake do not lose those 8 pages
> or you will ruin me in *time* lost and other things. If you find it answers please show
> to Mr Crookes; if not—answer me I am a fool—as usual, and then send back both
> those 8 pages and Mohini's *Memoir*. I MUST send it to Adyar to Olcott.[70]

From H.P.B.'s letter to Col. Olcott, dated October 21, we not only learn a
number of interesting facts about the work in progress but gather new and
rather curious information about the mailing of still another portion of the
manuscripts to Adyar. H.P.B. writes:

> Just a *month* ago, I gave to Mme Gebhard the MSS. of S.D. to post from
> Elberfeld—insuring it for 3,000 marks. Well, last night as you wrote to me that it had
> not been received till now, I telegraphed to her to ask whether she had not sent it
> (she had asked me to copy some things, before sending it) and she answered she *was
> going to*. Well after what you say of S.R. that he wont look at it even, of course it is
> better it should be printed without his approbation; for I want to begin this spring and
> will go to London for it. *Have to*—because of the proofreading, and the British
> Museum, and books. But now what shall I do for the 2nd Volume, the beginning
> of the true Archaic Doctrine—where I have any number of Sanskrit words and
> sentences, and the esoteric meaning of any number of exoteric Hindu allegories from
> their Cosmogony and Theogony? Can you ask Shrinivas Row and Bhavani Row to
> help me? Then I could send you the 2nd Vol. consisting of Books 1, 2 and 3. Unless
> someone helps I do not know what to do. And who will make the glossary? I can't
> and have no time, and Mohini hardly will. Please answer immediately. The whole
> almost is given by the 'old gentleman' and Master and there *are* wonderful things
> there I tell you. But someone must see to the Sanskrit and the corrections of the
> *exoteric* rendering. This book *will* make our future (yours and mine) see if it won't.
> Meanwhile I have written to Mme Gebhard to send the MSS. of Vol. I back
> here and not to send it to Adyar. It does seem useless since Subba R. is no more to
> be hoped for. Well, I will say nothing more.[71]

---

[70] *Letters to Sinnett*, Letter No. CII, pp. 224-25.

[71] Transcribed from the original in the Adyar Archives.

Whatever may have been the full and detailed story about the sending of the early manuscripts to Adyar—a story which we shall probably never have in its completeness because of paucity of documentary evidence—the actual manuscript at present in the Adyar Archives is a very interesting document.

It is in the handwriting of Countess Constance Wachtmeister and Mary Gebhard, some of the Stanzas being written *in red ink* as had been suggested by the Countess. It opens with a section headed 'To the Reader', the first paragraph of which begins: 'Error runs down on an inclined plane, while Truth has to laboriously climb its way up hill.'

It should be pointed out that available facts show that, whatever manuscripts were mailed to Adyar in 1886 or 1887, copies of *some of them* were kept by H.P.B. They were with her in London in later years. When some of her miscellaneous writings, then still unpublished, were gathered together and published in 1897 under the title 'The Secret Doctrine, Vol. III', this volume included a considerable number of sections which are either identical, or nearly so, with some of the chapters in the so-called Original Draft now at Adyar. It appears that those responsible for the so-called 'Volume III' were totally unaware of the existence of this material at Adyar, as is conclusively proved by the following facts.

The following statement may be found in the pages of *The Theosophist:*

> Another interesting 'find' is the first manuscript of the first volume of *The Secret Doctrine.* ... This evidently is the manuscript which H.P.B. sent from Ostende in 1886 to T. Subba Row. *The Secret Doctrine*, as we now have it, is an expanded version of this first manuscript, though in the later revision some sections are omitted which are in the original draft.[72]

The *Introductory* part of the 'Original Draft' (or 'First Draft') was expanded in the published work issued in 1888. Section I, Chapter I, dealt with the hermetic and other books of antiquity. Section II, 'White and Black Magic, in Theory and Practice', had been published as 'The Denials and the Mistakes of the Nineteenth Century', in *Lucifer*, Vol. X, June 1892, and, strangely enough, was used in 'Volume III'. Section III, on transcendental Algebra and 'God revealed' characters in mystic names became Section X in 'Volume III', together with other material about mathematics and geometry. Other sub-sections, like those on the hexagon and central point, on who was the Adept of Tyana, on the Kabiri or Mystery Gods, and others, are all included in 'Volume III'. The invaluable material entitled 'The Star-Angel Worship in the

---

[72] Unsigned, but probably by Annie Besant, in *The Theosophist*, Vol. XLIII, March 1922, pp. 533-34.

Facsimile of a page from the manuscript of the first draft of Volume I
of *The Secret Doctrine* in the handwriting of Frau Mary Gebhard,
preserved in the Adyar Archives.

Roman Church, etc.' was published in *Lucifer*, Vol. II, July 1888, in other words still in H.P.B.'s lifetime; it was enlarged and enriched with additional notes.

The second part of the 1886 Manuscript is headed: The Secret Doctrine. Part I, Archaic Period. Chapter I, A Glimpse into Eternity. Cosmic Evolution in Seven Stages.

Section One is entitled 'Pages from Prehistoric Period', and opens with the words: 'An Archaic Manuscript, a collection of palm leaves made impermeable to water, fire and air, by some specific unknown process—is before the eye of the writer.' It then goes on immediately to the circle with the point in the centre, but does not mention the immaculate white disk. After twenty-four pages, the first stanza is given, and a general glossary is promised for each chapter of an attached appendix. The notes on each stanza are put as footnotes, not in the text, as is the case in the final version of the printed work in 1888. The commentary on this stanza opens with: 'The Secret Doctrine postulates three fundamental propositions', words which occur in the final version on page 14 of Vol. I. Then follows the text which became the Commentaries in the published work, and all the notes on each stanza are given sequentially and not sloka by sloka.

Of Volume or Book II, only a few pages are in the manuscript, nineteen in all. They are headed: 'Archaic Chronology, Cycles, Anthropology', and are partly the rough cast of the 'Preliminary Notes' of the published work, and partly a brief indication of the line of teaching about chronology and races with which the volume is to deal.

On 10 December 1886, Col. Olcott's entry in his diary says that the Manuscripts of the *S.D.* have been received. And in his *Old Diary Leaves* (Series III, p. 385), he writes the following:

> About the same time I received from H.P.B. for reading and revision by T. Subba Row and myself, the MS. of Vol. I of the *Secret Doctrine*; but in his then captious mood the former refused to do more than read it, saying that it was so full of mistakes that if he touched it he should have to rewrite it altogether! This was mere pique, but did good, for when I reported his remark to H.P.B. she was greatly distressed, and set to work and went over the MS. most carefully, correcting many errors due to slipshod literary methods, and with the help of European friends making the book what it is now.

In his annual address at the Adyar Convention delivered on 27 December 1886, the Colonel said:

> The MSS. of the first volume has been sent me, and is undergoing revision. It will gratify you to learn that it more than maintains her reputation for learning and

(without a parent)[8]

Commentary on Stanza I.

[In order not to break the Stanzas by making the comments too long, the reader is referred for further explanations to the glossary in the Appendices attached to every chapter.]

The Secret Doctrine postulates three propositions:—
(a) An Omnipresent, Eternal & boundless Principle, beyond the reach of words or thought, or in the words of Mandukya "unthinkable & unspeakable." In the Aitareya Upanishad this Principle is referred to as the Self. the only one as just shown.

(b) The Eternity of the Universe as a fixed abstraction, with periodical appearances & disappearances of objective manifestation; like a regular tidal ebb of flux & reflux; coeval with, as being in one sense identical with the One Principle.

(c) The unity of all the Souls with the Over Soul or the unknown Root, & the continuous transmigration of each ray of the One infinite Light, in accordance with cyclic & Karmic Laws, during the whole cycle of Necessity; that is to say from the beginning of Manvantara to that of Pralaya, the Mayavic "Self" starting as a pure Emanation and returning as a purified Paramarthika Self, merged in the One Being (or non-Being)—the absolute "Paramartika." ✕

In its absolute abstraction, the One Principle though seemingly dual (Parabrahman & Mulaprakriti) is sexless, unconditioned, absolute. Its periodical radiation is, as a primal Emanation One, and androgynous & finite. When the "radiation" radiates in its turn, all the Secondary radiations are also androgynous to become male & female principles in their lower aspects. Pralaya is when the great or the minor, which leaves things status quo — the first that reawakens

✢ The "Eye of Siva", the inner or spiritual Eye of the Seer or clairvoyant.
✝ Daogma - a purified Soul, "the highest adept." ✠ Mayavic Self is the term given to the divine Ego of man, who labours under a delusion & he mistakes his Self as separated from the One Self, the absolute. Nevertheless it is his own, individual & impersonal Self throughout the Manvantaric eternities that returns into the absolute Self, like a drop of water into its Ocean, to re-emerge from it at the following Manvantara.

∥ It is not the physical, organised body that remains status quo, nor even the Soul of things during the great Cosmic or even Solar Pralayas, but only their akasic dual or photograph. But during the planetary or minor pralayas, once overreached by the night, the planets remain intact though dead, "like a huge animal caught between the polar ices stands frozen for ages."

Facsimile of a solitary page of one version of *The Secret Doctrine*
in H. P. B.'s handwriting preserved in the Adyar Archives.

literary ability. The work will probably extend to five volumes, of about the size of a
volume of *Isis Unveiled*, and the first, or Introductory, volume shortly be published at
London and New York.[73]

Similar information is contained in his closing address on the opening of
the Adyar Library, which was given December 28:

> And now, before closing, permit me one moment to announce that the entire
> MSS. of the first of five volumes that Madame Blavatsky is now writing upon the
> Secret Doctrine, is in my hands; and that even a cursory reading has satisfied better
> critics than myself that it will be one of the most important contributions ever made
> to philosophical and scientific scholarship, a monument of the learned author, and a
> distinction to the Adyar Library, of which she is one of the founders.[74]

The year 1887 opens with a letter written by H.P.B. to Col. Olcott on
January 4. It would seem that Subba Row liked at least portions of the work,
even if he had unyielding prejudices with regard to others. She writes:

> I am glad Subba Row likes my *Proem*. But it is *only* as *Preliminary* Vol. and
> the real, original doctrine is in the Volume I will send you when Fawcett comes on
> the 20th and then he will take it to England himself—for I cannot send it or rather
> *insure* it from here.
>
> So keep the other MSS. till you have read both and see what changes to make.
> Let S.R. do what he likes. I give him *carte blanche*. I trust in his wisdom far more
> than in mine, for I may have misunderstood in many a point both Master and the Old
> G.[75] They give me facts only and rarely dictate in succession. I am *no maker* of
> books you know it. But I know that my facts are all original and new. Wait and see..

---

[73] *The Theosophist*, Vol. VIII, Suppl. to January 1887. pp. xx-xxi.   [74] Ibid., p. xlvii.

[75] This stands for 'the Old Gentleman'. Letter 24 in the Second Series of *Letters from the Masters
of the Wisdom*, transcribed and annotated by C. Jinarājadāsa (Adyar: Theos. Publishing
House, 1925), is the only one in the handwriting of this Adept who signed himself with a
special script. The letter, written in red pencil, is preserved in the Archives of the
Theosophical Society at Adyar, and is reproduced in facscimile in the above-mentioned work.
Under the signature in script, there are a few words in H.P.B.'s handwriting and in blue
pencil. She says: 'the old gentleman your Narayan'. She also mentions him several times in
her brief *Diaries* of 1878 (See Volume I of her *Collected Writings*). This Adept was
apparently living near the Tiruvallam Hills in southern India, to judge by his forceful article
entitled 'A Mental Puzzle' which appeared in the Supplement to *The Theosophist* for June
1882 (Volume III) and was signed 'One of the Hindu Founders of the Parent Theosophical
Society'.
On 30 April 1882, H.P.B. and Col. Olcott went by rail to Tiruvallam, ostensibly to visit one of the oldest
temples of southern India. From various statements made by early members, they most likely met 'the
old gentleman' while in the vicinity. (See page 2 of the Supplement referred to above, as well as G.
Subiah Chetty's recollections in *The Theosophist*, Vol. XLVII, March 1926.)
The role played by this Adept in the writing of *Isis Unveiled* is beautifully drawn by Col. Olcott in the First
Series of his *Old Diary Leaves*, pp. 247-49. From H.P.B.'s own entries in her brief *Diaries* it appears
conclusively that at various times she acted as *tulku* for the 'old gentleman'.

Have you received the three gold things I sent? The Countess sent them on the same day as the MSS.[76]

On January 10, we find H.P.B. writing to Sinnett:

You want to know what I am doing? Atoning for my Sin of having sent to you my *Archaic Doct.* before it was ready. Rewriting it, adding to it, pasting and re-pasting, scratching out and replacing with notes from my AUTHORITIES. I was told to send you the MSS.—but not told when. The Countess who is always on the look out for practical things, wanting to profit through Hamilton going back to London—made me send with him the MSS. Two days after I was asked for it, and when I said it had gone was answered 'so much the worse for you'—thanks. It appears that in its crude state it failed to make Mr Crookes faint with rapture and he must have pronounced it a full blown flapdoodle. At least I augur it so and surmise, considering the *chemical* changes produced in it, in which neither before nor now do I understand one rap. Nor do I care.[77]

She also tells him in another letter of approximately the same time that *The Secret Doctrine* 'grows, grows and grows'.

In still another letter to Sinnett, she tells him: 'I am on the 4th Race. I have done with the Hermaphrodite Third Race.'

In the last week of March 1887, H.P.B. was gravely ill at Ostend, with a kidney infection which caused her to be unconscious for hours at a time. Dr Ashton Ellis came from London, and Mary Gebhard from Elberfeld. She was not expected to live. In the words of Countess Wachtmeister:

I hardly dared hope that she would live through the night, and while I was sitting alone by her bedside she opened her eyes and told me how glad she was to die, and that she thought the Master would let her be free at last. Still she was very anxious about her *Secret Doctrine.* I must be most careful of her manuscripts and hand all over to Col. Olcott with directions to have them printed. She had hoped that she would have been able to give more to the world, but the Master knew best. And so she talked on at intervals, telling me many things. At last she dropped off into a state of unconsciousness, and I wondered how it would all end.[78]

During the night, while the Countess was asleep, H.P.B.'s Teacher came to her at a time of grave crisis, and restored her failing health. In reply to the Countess' anxious inquiry, H.P.B. said:

Yes, Master has been here; he gave me my choice, that I might die and be free if I would, or I might live and finish *The Secret Doctrine.* He told me how great

---

[76] Transcribed from the original in the Adyar Archives.

[77] *Letters to Sinnett*, Letter No. CIV, pp. 226-27.

[78] *Reminiscences*, p. 73.

would be my sufferings and what a terrible time I would have before me in England (for I am to go there); but when I thought of those students to whom I shall be permitted to teach a few things, and of the Theosophical Society in general, to which I have already given my heart's blood, I accepted the sacrifice, and now to make it complete, fetch me some coffee and something to eat, and give me my tobacco box.[79]

Even in the midst of crises, H.P.B. preserved inviolate her sense of humour!

At this point in the story we have to introduce two new witnesses, namely, Bertram Keightley and his nephew, Dr Archibald Keightley, both of London, who have many interesting facts to relate. Bertram Keightley writes:

> During the few days I then spent at Ostend with H.P.B., she asked me to look over parts of the MSS. of her new work, which I gladly consented to do. Before I had read much it grew plain that *The Secret Doctrine* was destined to be by far the most important contribution of this century to the literature of Occultism; though even the inchoate and fragmentary character of much of the work led me to think that careful revision and much rearrangement would be needed before the manuscript would be fit for publication.
>
> On a second visit a week or two later, this impression was confirmed by further examination; but as H.P.B. then consented to come and settle in or near London as soon as arrangements could be made for her reception, nothing further was done about it at the time.[80]

This was before H.P.B.'s serious illness at Ostend.

The testimony of Dr Archibald Keightley is similar and refers to his experiences on a visit to H.P.B. at Ostend. He writes:

> Very soon after arriving I was handed a part of the MSS with a request to emendate, excise, alter the English, punctuate, in fact treat it as my own, a privilege I naturally did not avail myself of. The MSS. was then in detached sections, similar to those included under the heads of 'Symbolism' and 'Appendices' in the published volumes. What I saw was a mass of MSS. with no definite arrangement, much of which had been patiently and industriously copied by the Countess Wachtmeister. The idea then was to keep one copy in Europe, while the other went to India for correction by various native collaborators. The greater part did go at a later date, but some cause prevented the collaboration.
>
> What struck me most in the part I was able to read during my short stay was the enormous number of quotations from various authors. I knew that there was no library to consult and I could see that H.P.B.'s own books did not amount to thirty in all, of which several were dictionaries and several works counted two or more

---

[79] Ibid., p. 75.   [80] Ibid., pp. 89-90.

volumes. At this time I did not see the *Stanzas of Dzyan*, though there were several pieces of the *Occult Catechism* included in the MSS.

At a later date I again went to Ostend to carry out the arrangements for bringing H.P.B. to England. The main difficulty was to get her papers and books packed up. No sooner was one packed than it was wanted for reference; if part of the MSS. were put in a box it was certain to be that part which already contained some information which had to be cut out and placed elsewhere: and as H.P.B. continued to write until the very day before her departure, such was her unflagging industry, it was not easy matter to get her belongings packed.[81]

On 1 May 1887, H.P.B. moved over to London, first to 'Maycot', Crown-hill, Upper Norwood, and about September to 17 Lansdowne Road, Holland Park.

Bertram Keightley writes as follows with regard to this early period in London:

A day or two after our arrival at Maycot, H.P.B. placed the whole of the so-far completed MSS. in the hands of Dr (Archibald) Keightley and myself, instructing us to read, punctuate, correct the English, alter, and generally treat it as if it were our own—which we naturally did *not* do, having far too high an opinion of her knowledge to take any liberties with so important a work.

But we both read the whole mass of MSS.—a pile over three feet high—most carefully through, correcting the English and punctuation where absolutely indispensable, and then, after prolonged consultation, faced the author in her den—in my case with sore trembling, I remember—with the solemn opinion that the whole of the matter must be rearranged on some definite plan, since as it stood the book was another *Isis Unveiled*, only far worse, so far as absence of plan and consecutiveness were concerned.

After some talk, H.P.B. told us to go to Tophet and do what we liked. She had had more than enough of the blessed thing, had given it over to us, washed her hands thereof entirely, and we might get out of it as best we could.

We retired and consulted. Finally we laid before her a plan, suggested by the character of the matter itself, viz., to make the work consist of four volumes, each divided into three parts: (1) the Stanzas and Commentaries thereon; (2) Symbolism; (3) Science. Further, instead of making the first volume to consist, as she had intended, of the history of some great Occultists, we advised her to follow the natural order of exposition, and begin with the Evolution of Cosmos, to pass from that to the Evolution of Man, then to deal with the historical part in a third volume treating of the lives of some great Occultists; and finally, to speak of Practical Occultism in a fourth volume should she ever be able to write it.

This plan was laid before H.P.B., and it was duly sanctioned by her.

---

[81] Wachtmeister, *Reminiscences*, pp. 97-98.

The next step was to read the MSS. through again and make a general rearrangement of the matter pertaining to the subjects coming under the heads of Cosmogony and Anthropology, which were to form the first two volumes of the work. When this had been completed, and H.P.B. duly consulted, and her approval of what had been done obtained, the whole of the MSS. so arranged was typewritten out by professional hands, then re-read, corrected, compared with the original MSS., and all Greek, Hebrew, and Sanskrit quotations inserted by us. It then appeared that the whole of the Commentary on the Stanzas did not amount to more than some twenty pages of the present work, as H.P.B. had not stuck closely to her text in writing. So we seriously interviewed her, and suggested that she should write a proper commentary, as in her opening words she had promised her reader to do. Her reply was characteristic: 'What on earth am I to say? What *do* you want to know? Why it's all as plain as the nose on your face!!!' We could not see it; she didn't—or made out she didn't—so we retired to reflect. ... I think the removal to Lansdowne Road [had been] effected, before the problem of the Commentary on the Stanzas was finally solved.

The solution was this:—Each sloka of the stanzas was written (or cut out from the typewritten copy) and pasted at the head of a sheet of paper, and then on a loose sheet pinned thereto were written all the questions we could find time to devise upon that sloka. In this task Mr Richard Harte helped us very considerably, a large proportion of the questions put being of his devising. H.P.B. struck out large numbers of them, made us write fuller explanations, or our own ideas—such as they were—of what her readers expected her to say, wrote more herself, incorporated the little she had already written on that particular sloka, and so the work was done.

But when we came to think of sending the MSS. to the printers, the result was found to be such that the most experienced compositor would tear his hair in blank dismay. Therefore Dr Keightley and myself set to work with a typewriter, and alternately dictating and writing, made a clean copy of the first parts of Volumes I and II.

Then work was continued till parts II and III of each volume were in a fairly advanced condition, and we could think of sending the work to press.

It had originally been arranged that Mr George Redway should publish the work, but his proposals not being financially satisfactory, the needful money was offered by a friend of H.P.B.'s, and it was resolved to take the publication of *Lucifer* into our own hands. So the Duke Street office was taken, and business begun there the primary object being to enable the T.S. to derive the utmost possible benefit from H.P.B.'s writings.

Of the further history of *The Secret Doctrine* there is not much more to say—though there were months of hard work before us. H.P.B. read and corrected two sets of galley proofs, then a page proof, and finally a revised in sheet, correcting, adding, and altering up to the very last moment:—result: printer's bill for corrections alone over £ 300.[82]

---

[82] Ibid., 90-95.

To this may be added the following excerpt on the same subject, this time in the words of Dr Archibald Keightley:

The Secret Doctrine began to be printed and in this and in *Lucifer* Mme Blavatsky's idiosyncrasy of regarding page proof as being equivalent to manuscript, led to much argument and expense. It was not merely that she would divide a page after the type was all locked in the forms and insert a quantity of fresh matter, but she would with much care and precision of scissors cut out and then paste in a single sentence in an entirely different place. Woe betide the zealous sub-editor who protested on behalf of the printers and the provision of funds. 'Off with his head' or his metaphysical scalp were the orders of the Queen of our wonderland. Nevertheless the account for corrections of *The Secret Doctrine* came to more than the original cost of setting up! [83]

Elsewhere, Dr Archibald Keightley, writing about his experiences after H.P.B. had moved to London, says:

All through that summer Bertram Keightley and I were engaged in reading, re-reading, copying and correcting. The last amounted to casting some of the sentences in English mould, for many of them were 'literal translations from the French'. One remarkable fact is worth noticing. It was not long before the *genius loci* became apparent and in most of the MSS. written after the date of arrival in England there was very little of this kind of correction needed.

Many of the quotations had to be verified, and here we should have been lost if it had not been for a hint from H.P.B. She told us one night that sometimes in writing down quotations, which for the purpose of the book had been impressed on the Astral Light before her, she forgot to reverse the figures—for instance page 123 would be allowed to remain 321 and so on. With this in mind verification was easier, for one was puzzled on examining all editions in the British Museum to find in several cases that the books did not contain the number of pages. With the reversal matters were straightened out and the correct places found.

Much of the MSS. was typewritten at this period. This was H.P.B.'s opportunity. The spaces were large and much could be inserted. Needless to say, it was. The thick type-MSS. were cut, pasted, recut and pasted several times over, until several of them were twice the size of the original MSS. But in it all was apparent that no work and no trouble, no suffering or pain could daunt her from her task. Crippled with rheumatism, suffering from a disease which had several times nearly proved fatal, she still worked unflaggingly, writing at her desk the moment her eyes and fingers could guide the pen. ...

During the greater part of the period in London H.P.B. had the assistance of E.D. Fawcett, especially in those parts of the second volume dealing with the

---

[83] 'Reminiscences of H.P. Blavatsky', *The Theosophical Quarterly*, Vol. VII, October 1910.

evolutionary hypotheses. He suggested, corrected, and wrote, and several pages of his MSS. were incorporated by H.P.B. into her work.

Needless to say our work went on. We had to carry the general scheme. ... in our heads. We had to draw H.P.B.'s attention to the repetitions occurring in the isolated sections, and so far as possible in this way to act as watchdogs and help her to make the meaning as clear as possible. But all the work was hers. A few stops here and there, a few suggestions, the correction of a French-spelled word, was ours; the rest was H.P.B.'s own, and all was approved by her. ...

. . . Failing health and strength came, and it was an increasing task to rise so early or to work so late. Still time continued and work went on, and the estimates of printers were examined. Certain requirements as to size of page and margin were peculiar points with H.P.B., as also were the thickness and quality of paper. Some of her critics had disliked the thickness of *Isis Unveiled*, so the paper had to be thinner so as to reduce the size. These points decided, the book began to go to press. It so happened that I was called into the country and so did not see the first half or more of the first volume as it passed. But it went through three or four other hands besides H.P.B.'s in galley proof, as well as in revise. She was her own most severe corrector, and was liable to treat revise as MSS., with alarming results in the correction item in the bill.

Then came the writing of the preface, and finally the book was out. The period of work and excitement was over and all was quiet till the first copy was delivered.[84]

Substantially the same information is given by Bertram Keightley in his *Reminiscences of H.P.B.*, but with the following very important additional point:

When we had got all the MS. typed out, we tied up the original MS. complete *as it was* and made a strong sealed parcel of it all, which was given back to H.P.B., and was subsequently removed to No. 19 Avenue Road, St John's Wood, N.W. (Mrs Besant's house) when H.P.B. moved there. I clearly remember seeing the parcel there intact shortly before I left for India a few months before H.P.B.'s death.[85]

This information is of special interest. It is a great pity that nobody seems to have any idea what eventually became of this package. It does not appear to be in any present-day theosophical archives. Many uncertainties about the *S.D.* might have been cleared up if it were possible to consult this MS. It is quite possible also that some of its pages were in precipitated handwriting. It merely underlines the total lack of any historical sense on the part of Theosophists of that era.

---

[84] Wachtmeister, *Reminscences*, pp. 98-100.
[85] Adyar, Madras; Theosophical Publishing House, 1931, p. 13.

Writing in his *Old Diary Leaves*, Series IV, p. 22, Col. Olcott speaks of the grievances of the year 1887, and says, among other things:

... the refusal of Subba Row to edit the *Secret Doctrine* MSS., contrary to his original promise, although she [H.P.B.] had had it type-copied at a cost of £ 80 and sent me for that purpose.

Of this typescript we have no further information. The manuscript in the Adyar Archives covers 229 foolscap pages in the handwriting of the Countess and Mary Gebhard, and no typewritten manuscripts are known to exist. It would not be possible to specify what particular material was typewritten, or what became of this typescript. The refusal on the part of Subba Row, however, is quite definite.

On 10 September 1887, H.P.B. writing to her staunch friend G. Subiah Chetty confirms two points already mentioned. She says:

... Subba Row has even refused through C. Oakley to read or have anything to do [with] my *Secret Doctrine*. I have spent here £ 30 to have it typed, on purpose to send to him and now when all is ready, he refuses to look into it. Of course it will be a new pretext for him to pitch into and criticise when it does come out. Therefore I will defer its publication.[86]

At the Annual Convention held at Adyar 27-29 December 1887, the President-Founder reported that:

During the past twelve months she [H.P.B.] has sent me the MSS. of four out of the probable five volumes of 'The Secret Doctrine' for examination, and it is expected that the first volume will issue at London during the coming spring season.[87]

Uncertainties arising as a result of the above statements may never be fully cleared up at this late date.

We must not overlook Col. Olcott's outspoken praise of the Keightleys and their devoted help. Writing in *The Theosophist*, the Colonel stated:

The devotion of Mr Keightley as well as of Dr. Archibald Keightley to the work of the Society, and especially to Madame Blavatsky, during the past four years, has been most conspicuous and won for them general respect. Both university graduates and young men of ample fortune, they have eschewed the pleasures which the world offers to those who are similarly situated, to take up the hard, and unrequited drudgery of Headquarters work with an enthusiasm hard to find even in the best paid

---

[86] Transcribed from the original in the Adyar Archives.

[87] *The Theosophist*, Vol. IX, Supple. to January, 1888, p.xvii

employees. Mr Bertram Keightley advanced the money which it cost to bring out *The Secret Doctrine*, and did many other acts of generosity.[88]

The year 1888 opened with the receipt of a letter sent to H.P.B. from New York and signed by a number of American Theosophists, protesting against the attitude of certain Indian pundits towards her work.[89]

The following letter has been sent to Madame Blavatsky from New York. It is not intended to reflect upon the East Indians as a body in any way; but solely to show why the signers desire that *The Secret Doctrine* should not be held back because some Indian pundits are against it.—[Editor, *The Path*].

NEW YORK, January 19, 1888.

MADAME H.P. BLAVATSKY,

RESPECTED CHIEF:—We have just heard that you have been asked to withdraw from publication *The Secret Doctrine*.

This extraordinary request emanates, we are told, from members of the Theosophical Society, who say that if the book is brought out it will be attacked or ridiculed by some East Indian pundits, and that it is not wise to antagonize these Indian gentlemen.

We most earnestly ask you not to pay heed to this desire, but to bring out *The Secret Doctrine* at the earliest possible day.

It is a work for which we, and hundreds of others all over the United States, have been waiting for some years, most of us standing firmly on the promise made by yourself that it was being prepared and would appear.

While the West has the highest regard for the East Indian philosophy, it is, at the same time, better able to grasp and understand works that are written by those acquainted with the West, with its language, with its usages and idiom, and with its history, and who are themselves westerners. As we well know that it is from the West the chief strength of the Theosophical Society is to come, although its knowledge and inspiration may and do reach us from the East, we are additionally anxious that you, who have devoted your life to this cause and have hitherto granted us the great boon found in *Isis Unveiled*, should not now stop almost at the very point of giving us *The Secret Doctrine*, but go on with it in order that we may see your pledge fulfilled and another important stone laid in the Theosophical edifice.

Further, we hasten to assure you that it makes but small difference—if any whatever—here in the vast and populous West what any one or many pundits in India say or threaten to say about *The Secret Doctrine*, since we believe that although a great inheritance has been placed before the East Indians by their ancestors they have not seized it, nor have they in these later days given it out to their fellow men living beyond the bounds of India, and since this apathy of theirs, combined with

---

[88] Vol. XI, Suppl. to April, 1890, p. cxxi.
[89] *The Path*, New York, Vol. II, February 1888, pp. 354-55.

MARY GEBHARD
From a contemporary oil painting, courtesy of Madame
Marie-Josephe Gebhard-L'Estrange.

19 AVENUE ROAD, LONDON, ENGLAND

H. P. B. resided in this house from July, 1890,
to the time of her death, May 8, 1891.

their avowed belief that all Western people, being low-caste men, cannot receive the Sacred Knowledge, has removed these pundits from the field of influence upon Western thought.

And lastly, knowing that the great wheel of time has turned itself once more so that the Powers above see that the hour has come when to all people, East and West alike, shall be given the true knowledge, be it Vedantic or otherwise, we believe that the Masters behind the Theosophical Society and whom you serve, desire that such books as *The Secret Doctrine* should be written.

We therefore earnestly entreat you not to be moved from your original purpose and plain pledge that, before passing away from our earthly sight, you would lay before us *The Secret Doctrine*.

Receive, Madame, the assurances of our high esteem and the pledge of our continued loyalty.

Signed:

WILLIAM Q. JUDGE	MRS J.G. GRIFFIN
J. CAMPBELL VER PLANCK	ALEX O. DRAGICSEVICS
SAMUEL HICKS CLAPP	E. H. SANBORN
ALEXANDER FULLERTON	E. M. TOZIER
EDSON D. HAMMOND	E. DAY MACPHERSON
ABNER DOUBLEDAY	JNO. F. MILLER, M.D.
GEORGE W. WHEAT	WILLIAM M. GATES
JNO. W. LOVELL	EMILY G. FLEMING
GEORGE W. SALTER	E. B. GRAY, JR.
LYDIA BELL	HADJI ERINN, for himself and 26 others

In June a letter to the Editor of *The Path*, dated from Bombay and signed by a number of Indian pundits protested against the idea expressed in the February *Path* on the subject of the publication of the *S.D.*

TO THE EDITOR OF 'THE PATH' :

Dear Sir and Brother —In the February number of *The Path* you have published a letter written by several American Theosophists to our respected Founder, Madame Blavatsky, asking her to hasten the publication of *The Secret Doctrine*, which, it is alleged, has not come out yet because some Indian pundits are against it.

It seems to us that the letter has been based upon information which is not correct. Had Madame Blavatsky been in India, the book would long ago have seen the light. Owing, however, to her stay in Europe, it has not been found so very easy to have the great work revised, as had been originally proposed.

Parts of the work were sent to this country, when some good suggestions were made with a view to enhance the value of the book by making it more exact in its allusions to Hindu literature. These suggestions were misunderstood by some who

4

communicated their own views on the matter to Europe, and we fear Madame Blavatsky herself has not been properly informed in what way the revision was proposed to be effected. Had she herself been here, she would, with her usual candor and good sense, have at once understood the situation and cheerfully taken up the well-meant suggestions. Occult ideas and doctrines ought to be made to stand on their own intrinsic merits, and not on the authority of any person or persons; and as there is a possibility of making this truly marvellous work more acceptable to the public, more useful and instructive, we hope and trust that the suggestions that have been made will be carried out.

There is no opposition here against the publication of the mysteries of occultism. A few sympathetic friends can easily arrange to have the work revised, if the false impressions produced by unfounded reports were forgotten and the work placed in the hands of those who are capable of revising it.

Yours fraternally,

N. D. Khandalavala	J. N. Isaac
Rustomji Ardeshir Master	Pherozshaw Rustomji Mehta
Tookaram Tatya	Rustomji K. Modi
Shamarár Vithal	Pestonje Nouroji Pavdi, *G.G.M. College*
J.C. Dorabji	Ardeshir Sorabji, *Engineer*
Manchershá Kavasji	Cowasji Dossàbhoy Davar
K.M. Shroff	N.E. Bilimorià
Hamra Rustomji	Framjee B. Bilimorià

Bombay, India,
April 1988.

Much light is thrown on certain prevailing attitudes in India by H.P.B.'s letter of 24 February 1888, written to Col. Olcott. She says:

Now Tookaram writes me a letter. In it he says that S. R. told him he was ready to help me and correct my *S. D. provided* I took out from it every reference to the Masters! Now, what's this? Does he mean to say that I should *deny* the Masters, or that I do not understand Them and garble the facts They give me, or that *he*, S.R., knows Master's doctrines better than I do? For it can mean all this. Please take your first opportunity of telling the whole of Adyar as follows:

(1) It is *I*, who brought in, the first, the existence of our Masters to the world and the T.S. I did it because They sent me to do the work and make a fresh experiment in this XIX Century and I have done it, the best I knew how. It may not dovetail with S.R.'s ideas, it answers truth and fact. ... And one of the two—I *either know Them personally as I have ever maintained;* or—*I have invented Them and Their doctrines.*[90]

---

[90] Transcribed from the original in the Adyar Archives.

These contradictory views are not to be taken lightly. Appearances are proverbially deceptive. In order to understand the situation, at least to some extent, it is necessary to realize that the teachings which H.P.B. was giving out at the instruction of, and often, at the direct dictation of, her own superiors, cut across the lines of entrenched Brahmanical exclusiveness and aroused deep-seated jealousies and resentments among them.

An unsigned note in the May 1888 issue of *The Theosophist* (Suppl. to Vol. IX, p. xxxvii), most likely written by Bertram Keightley, informs the readers that:

> The publication of the 'Secret Doctrine' has been commenced, and, as soon as the magnitude and, of course, the cost of the work can be definitely calculated, the price to subscribers will be fixed and a circular sent them giving them the option of taking it or receiving back their money, which has been lying in the bank untouched ever since they paid it. The 'Secret Doctrine' is so vast a theme and ramifies into so many directions, that its treatment involves enormous labour, with no possibility of fixing in advance the number or size of the volumes required. Hence the necessity of revising the Manager's contract with the subscribers.

To this period belongs also a letter addressed by Mr Judge to Bertram Keightley dealing with several topics connected with the production of *The Secret Doctrine*. Its text is as follows:

JULY 21 [1888]

> My dear Keightley,
> I have taken the necessary steps for procuring copyright of *Secret Doctrine* and have filed the proper papers, paid the fees and obtained the regular certificates from the copyright office. Those certificates I enclose: please acknowledge the receipt.
> The sending of sheets to me which have been printed in Europe, does not invalidate or affect the copyright, as the law does not direct the *printing* to be done here; so, it may be done anywhere. If you desire another legal opinion hereupon, a remittance must be sent me as I have no money. It was all used up in those *crisis* telegrams which cost $ 40 & I am high and dry.
> Mr Parker remains silent so I do not now expect that money. The binding will be only about 50c per vol. here & I have over $ 100 subscribed and a lot of subscriptions registered which will be paid afterwards sure; so I think perhaps I will have enough to do the binding, etc., by the time the book is out. Can you tell me, *will* it be out in Oct. or Nov.?
> I must give dealers here 20% as that is the least they will accept & is much less than is usual.
> I do not think you need doubt but that the sale will be large, as there is a great interest in the book.
> I do not understand about Parker. He was very effusive and 5 times promised the $ 1,500 at once, but for 3 months hasn't squeaked.

I have written out West to try & discover what, if anything, is the matter with him.

Regards to all,
As ever,

Bertram Keightley, Esq.   William Q. Judge [91]

On 12 August 1888, Judge N. D. Khandalavala, writing from Ahmedabad, addressed a letter to the Editor of *The Path* (Vol. III, October 1888, pp. 233-34), the contents of which throw a flood of light upon the situation prevailing in India at the time:

Ahmedabad, India, 12th August, 1888.

To THE EDITOR OF THE PATH:

Dear Sir and Brother,

In the June number of your valuable Journal there has been published a letter, signed by myself and other Indian Theosophists, to the effect that, if Madame Blavatsky consented, her forthcoming great work would be revised by competent Hindu students in India who would be able to throw a great deal of light on Indian Philosophy. When that letter was written we were under the impression that a learned gentleman here, who had expressed his willingness to revise the 'Secret Doctrine' under certain conditions, would really do so. Myself and another friend represented all the facts to Madame Blavatsky, who at once agreed to place her volumes into the hands of the said Indian scholar and to abide by his conditions. For reasons, however, best known to himself, the said student of Indian Esoterism refused to undertake the task of revising the book or even parts of it.

Madame Blavatsky, therefore, can no longer be blamed for not taking the assistance of Indian scholars. Perhaps it is after all for the best that her marvellous and unique work should come out as originally written by herself.

I have thought fit to write these few lines lest our former letter might create some misunderstanding.

Yours fraternally,
N. D. KHANDALAVALA, F.T.S.

In the autumn of 1888, the following circular was printed for distribution. To judge by the address given in it, it must have been issued from London. The table of contents differs considerably from the one finally adopted.

---

[91] From one of the letter-press copybooks of Mr Judge held in the Archives of The Theosophical Society, Pasadena, California. Originally printed in *The Theosophical Forum* Vol. X. June 1937, pp. 423-24.

[IN THE PRESS]

To be published on or about October 27th, 1888, in Two Volumes, Royal Octavo, of circa 650 pp. each

---

THE SECRET DOCTRINE

THE SYNTHESIS OF SCIENCE, RELIGION AND PHILOSOPHY

BY

H.P. BLAVATSKY

AUTHOR OF 'ISIS UNVEILED'

With a copious Index and a Glossary of Terms

In all ages, and in all lands, the belief has existed that a Divine degree of knowledge is possible to human beings under certain conditions; and, as a corollary to this, the conviction has dwelt in the hearts of the people that living men exist who possess this knowledge—whether they be called sages, philosophers, adepts, or by any other name.

In ancient times this knowledge was taught and communicated in the 'Mysteries', of which traces have been found among all the nations of the earth, from Japan through China and India to America, and from the frozen north to the islands of the South Pacific.

In modern times the existence of this knowledge has been divined by different scholars and students, who have called it by various names, of which 'The Secret Wisdom' is one.

The author of this work has devoted more than forty years of her life to the study and acquisition of this knowledge; she has gained admittance as a student to some of the Secret Schools of this Wisdom, and has learnt to know and appreciate its extent and value.

The purpose of the present work, then, is to lay before the thinking world so much of this 'Hidden Wisdom' as it is thought expedient to make known at present to men in general.

In her earlier work, *Isis Unveiled*, the author dealt with Science and Theology from a critical standpoint. But little of the positive Esoteric teaching of the Secret Wisdom was there brought forward, though many hints and suggestions were thrown out. These will find a fuller explanation in the present volumes.

The publication of Mr Sinnett's *Esoteric Buddhism* was a first attempt to supplement the negative and purely critical attitude of *Isis Unveiled* by a positive and systematic scheme. The way has thus been prepared for this work; and the reader of the books just referred to will find those outlines, which were only sketched in the earlier presentations of the subject, filled in and elaborated in the two volumes now offered for his consideration.

The first of these volumes contains Book I of *The Secret Doctrine*, and is concerned mainly with the evolution of Kosmos. It is divided into three parts.

Part I commences with an introduction explaining the philosophical basis of the system. The skeleton of this book is formed by seven Stanzas, translated from the Secret Book of Dzyan, with commentary and explanations by the translator. This work is among the oldest MSS. in the world; it is written in the Sacred Language of the Initiates, and constitutes the text-book, which was the basis of the oral instruction imparted during the Mysteries.

A section of the work devoted to the consideration of the bearings of some of the views advanced upon modern science, follows the Stanzas. Some probable objections from this point of view are met by anticipation, and the scientific doctrines at present in vogue on these questions are considered and compared with those put forward in this work.

Part II is devoted to the elucidation of the fundamental symbols contained in the great religions of the world, particularly the Christian, the Hebrew, and the Brahmanical.

Part III forms the connecting link between Book I, which deals with the Genesis of Kosmos; and Book II (forming the second volume), which treats of the Evolution of Man.

The arrangement of Vol. II is similar to that of Vol.I.

Part I contains a series of Stanzas from the Book of Dzyan, which describe the Evolution of Humanity in our cycle. This is followed by a discussion of the scientific issues raised, with special reference to the modern hypothesis that man and the ape are descended from a common ancestor.

Part II embraces a series of chapters explaining the symbols typifying the evolutionary history of mankind in various religions, particularly the Biblical account of the Creation and Fall of Man given in *Genesis.*

Part III contains matter supplementary to Books I and II, dealing with questions which could not be previously discussed at adequate length without breaking the sequence of the narrative.

CONTENTS OF VOLUME I

BOOK 1—COSMOGENESIS

PART I

Introduction.—The Seven Stanzas from the Book of Dzyan, with Commentary and Explanations:—The Night of the Universe—The Awakening of Kosmos—The Beginnings of Differentiation—The Septenary Hierarchy of Divine Powers—Our World: Its Growth and Development—The Dawn of Humanity—Summary and Conclusion.

ADDENDUM

Reasons for this Addendum—Modern Physicists are Playing at Blind Man's Buff—An Lumen Sit Corpus An Non—Is Gravitation a Law?—The Theories of Rotation in Science—The Nature of Force and the Atom—The Scientific Theory of Force attacked by a Man of Science—Life-force or Gravity?—An Analysis of the So-called 'Elements' of Science—On the Elements and Atoms—Scientific and Esoteric Evidence for, and Objections to the Nebular Theory—Forces, Modes of Motion, or Intelligences—which?—Summary of the Respective Positions.

PART II

Explanatory Sections on Symbolism and the Eastern Presentation of the Secret Cosmography—Symbolism and Ideographs—The Mystery-Language—The Symbolism of the Cross and Circle—Primordial Substance and Divine Thought—Chaos, Theos, Kosmos—The Mundane Egg—The Hidden Deity: Its Symbols and Glyphs—The Lotus a Universal Symbol—Deus Lunus—Theogony of the Creators—The Seven Creations—The Monad and its Origin—Gods, Monads, and Atoms.

PART III

Narada and Asura Maya—The Chronology of the Brahmans—Exoteric and Esoteric Chronology—The Primeval *Manus* of Humanity—The Approximate Duration of Ages and Races—Calculations illustrating the Divisions—The Racial Divisions—The Seventh *Manu* and Our Mankind.

CONTENTS OF VOLUME II

BOOK II.—ANTHROPOGENESIS

PART I

Introduction.—1. On the Archaic Stanzas, and the Four Prehistoric Contents. 2. Anthropogenesis in the Secret Volume.

Section I.—General Evolution under the Guidance of the Seven Creators—Primeval Creations and Failures—Creation of Divine Beings in the Exoteric Accounts—Nature Unaided Fails—The Various Fabricators of Man—Various Primeval Modes of Procreation—The Three Primeval Races—Evolution of Animals from the Atoms of the Three Primeval Races.

Section II.—From the Divine down to the First Human Races—The Evolution and Involution of Man—The 'Fall'—Upon the Nature of the Sons of 'Dark Wisdom'—The 'Secret of Satan'—On the Identity and Difference of the Incarnating Powers—Ancient and Modern Views of Satan, and of the Astral Light: 'His abode'.

Section III.—A Panoramic View of the Early Races—On the Third Race after its Fall—etc., etc., etc.

Section IV.—On Ancient Submerged Continents—On the Original Lemuria and the Wisdom thereof—The Ancient Zodiacs, and what their Records Teach us—The Religion of the Prehistoric Races—The Divine Dynasties—The Giants of Atlantis—etc., etc.

Section V.—Giants, Civilizations, and Submerged Continents Traced in History—Statements about the Sacred Islands and Continents in the Classics Explained Esoterically—Western Speculations Founded on Greek and Purānic Accounts—Witnesses in Stone—Other Cyclopean Ruins and Colossal Stones as Witnesses to Giants—Concerning Edens, Serpents and Nagas—etc., etc., etc.

ADDENDUM

Human evolution according to modern science contrasted and compared with the teachings of Esoteric Science, etc., etc.

PART II

CHAPTERS ON SYMBOLISM

The Holy of Holies—The 'Sons of God' and the Sacred Island—'Adam-Adami' and other names—Nebo of Birs- Nimrod—etc., etc., etc.

INDEX AND GLOSSARY

Published at — £ 2 2s. 0d.   Subscription price —£ 1.8s.0d.

Names and addresses of subscribers in Europe, accompanied by the amount of the subscription, should be sent to the Manager, Mr B. Keightley, Theosophical Publishing Company, Limited, 7, Duke Street, Adelphi, London, W.C.; and in America to Mr W.Q. Judge, P.O. Box 2659, New York, on or before the date of publication.

....—........................

To

MR B. KEIGHTLEY,
THEOSOPHICAL PUBLISHING COMPANY, LIMITED,
7, Duke Street, Adelphi, London, W.C.

Sir,
Please receive herewith the sum of £ 1.8s., and enter my name as a Subscriber for one copy of the 'Secret Doctrine', to be forwarded to—

Name ....
Address ....
....
....

As has already been pointed out—a most important fact which bears repetition at this point—Col. Olcott, then on his way to Europe, received on 22 August 1888, on board the P. & O. Mail Steamer *Shannon*, a letter from the Master K.H. He had sailed from Bombay on August 7, and was then approaching Brindisi, Italy. The importance of certain words of the Master cannot be overestimated. The letter said:

> I have also noted your thoughts about the 'Secret Doctrine'. Be assured that what she has not *annotated* from scientific and other works, we have given or *suggested* to her. Every mistake or erroneous notion, corrected and explained by her from the works of other theosophists *was corrected by me, or under my instruction.* It is a more valuable work than its predecessor, an epitome of occult truths that will make it a source of information and instruction for the earnest student for long years to come.[92]

The October 1888 issue of *The Path* (Vol. III, p.233) published a notice concerning *The Secret Doctrine*, stating that:

---

[92] *Letters from the Masters of the Wisdom 1881-1888*, First Series, Letter No. XIX. Fourth edition, Adyar, Theosophical Publishing House, 1948.

It is fully expected that the first, and probably the second, volume of *The Secret Doctrine* will be ready for mailing about October 26th ... the privilege of securing it at the reduced rate ceases upon its issue.

In the same month, *The Theosophist* (Vol. X, Suppl. to October 1888, p. xviii), reporting on Col. Olcott's visit to Europe, informed the readers that H.P.B.:

...works at her writing desk from morning to night, preparing 'copy' and reading proofs for *The Secret Doctrine* and her London magazine, *Lucifer*. Of her greatest work over three hundred pages of each of the two volumes were already printed when Colonel Olcott arrived, and both Volumes will probably appear this month. From all he heard from competent judges who had read the manuscript, the President was satisfied that *The Secret Doctrine* will surpass in merit and interest even *Isis Unveiled*.

It would appear that sheets of the first volume, most likely folded and collated, were sent to W.Q. Judge in New York.

On 5 October 1888, Mr Judge, writing from New York to Bertram Keightley, informs him that:

The dummy is at hand. Shall be glad to get the sheets, but there is so much delay it will not be possible to have the book [*The Secret Doctrine*, American edition] out by 27th. Will try my best however. The book is splendid from the part found in the dummy. I get a few orders every week.

The prospectus you sent out from London has made bother, since you put the price £1.8 and I at $7.50. But I suppose you have sent out no more. I hope the index is good.[93]

In a letter of October 26, he tells him again:

The trouble I expected with the Appraiser [of the Custom House] came on. He sent for me after I had taken out 3 cases, and said that the book [*S.D.*] was undervalued. On a calculation it appeared that the 1000 copies came to some 30c each. This of course is too low, and therefore I was stared in the face with the chance of a penalty and double duty. The law is: that we must pay duty here (at 25%) upon the market value of the goods. In this case that is determined by cost of paper and printing; in the case of a book already sold the wholesale price abroad determines the value upon which duty is to be paid

---

[93] *Practical Occultism*, from the private letters of William Q. Judge, p.127 (Theosophical University Press, Pasadena, Calif., 1951).

§ Seven

To accomplish the proposed task, the writer had to resort to the rather unusual means of dividing each volume or Book into three Parts; the first of which only is the consecutive, though very fragmentary, history of the Cosmogony and the Evolution of Man on this globe. But these two volumes had to serve as a PROLOGUE, and prepare the reader's mind for those which shall now follow. In treating of Cosmogony and now of the Anthropogenesis of mankind, it was necessary to show that no religion, since the very earliest, has ever been entirely based on fiction, as none was the object of special revelation; and that it is dogma which has ever been killing primeval truth. Finally, that no human-born dogma, no institution, however sanctified by custom and antiquity, can compare in sacredness with the dogma of Nature. The Key of Wisdom that unlocks the massive gates leading to the arcana of the innermost sanctuaries can be found hidden in her bosom only; which is in the countries pointed to by the great seer of the past century, Emanuel Swedenborg. There lies the heart of nature, that bosom whence issued the early races of primeval Humanity, and which is the cradle of physical man.

Satyât Nâsti paro dharmah.

THERE IS NO RELIGION HIGHER THAN TRUTH.

END OF VOL. II

Thus far have proceeded the rough outlines of the Scriptural beliefs and tenets of the archaic, earliest Races contained in their hitherto Secret Scriptural records. But our explanations are by no means complete, nor do they pretend to give out the full text,

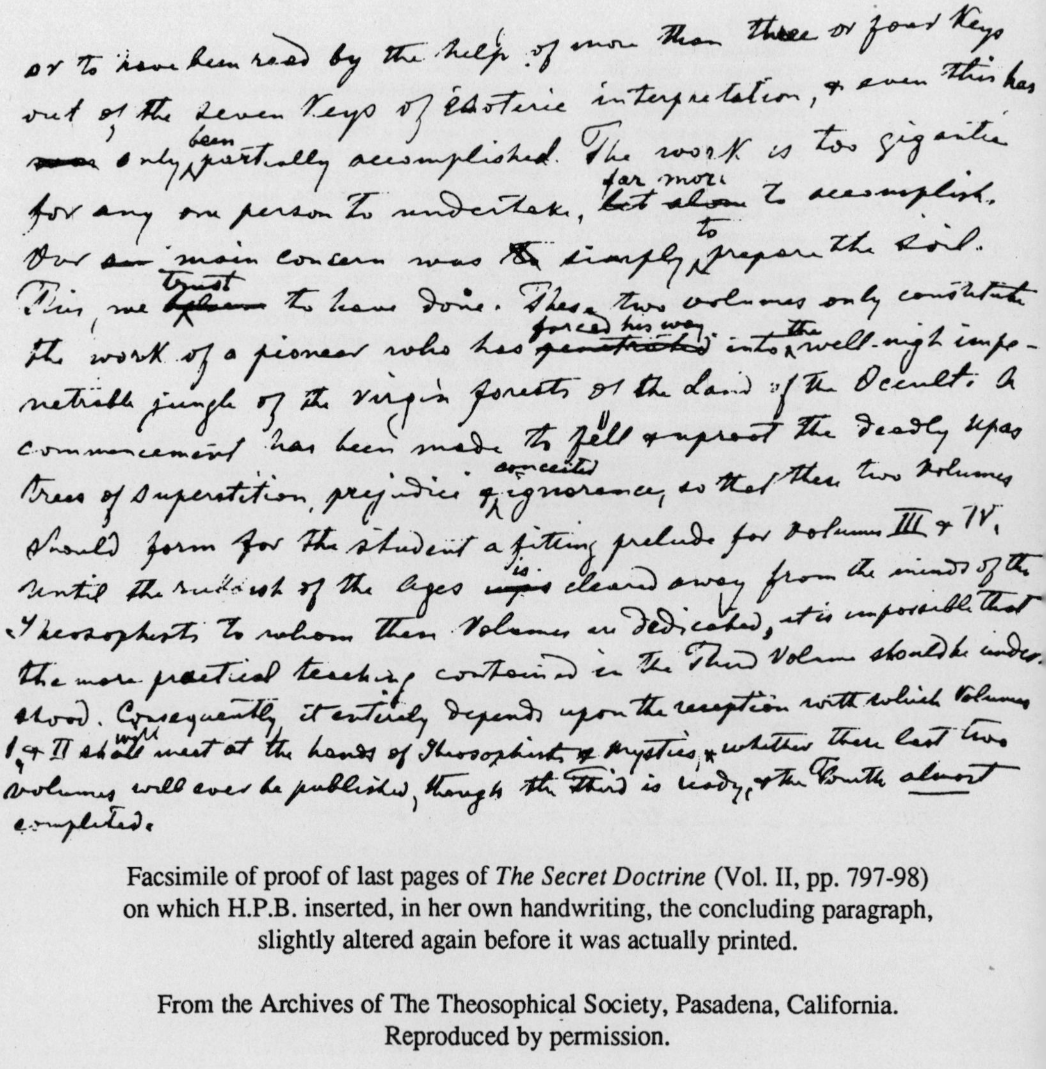

or to have been read by the help of more than three or four Keys out of the seven Keys of esoteric interpretation, & even this has only been partially accomplished. The work is too gigantic for any one person to undertake, far more to accomplish. Our main concern was simply to prepare the soil. This, we trust to have done. These two volumes only constitute the work of a pioneer who has forced his way into the well-nigh impenetrable jungle of the virgin forests of the Land of the Occult. A commencement has been made to fell & uproot the deadly upas trees of superstition, prejudice & conceited ignorance, so that these two volumes should form for the student a fitting prelude for Volumes III & IV. Until the rubbish of the ages is cleared away from the minds of the Theosophists to whom these Volumes are dedicated, it is impossible that the more practical teaching contained in the Third Volume should be understood. Consequently it entirely depends upon the reception with which Volumes I & II will meet at the hands of Theosophists & Mystics, whether these last two volumes will ever be published, though the third is ready, & the Fourth almost completed.

Facsimile of proof of last pages of *The Secret Doctrine* (Vol. II, pp. 797-98) on which H.P.B. inserted, in her own handwriting, the concluding paragraph, slightly altered again before it was actually printed.

From the Archives of The Theosophical Society, Pasadena, California. Reproduced by permission.

But after a long argument and great persuasion, and perhaps for other causes, the Appraiser consented to let the book through, with the caution that on the next invoice the true value is to be stated. When I see you I will have the minutest directions regarding 2nd vol.

It is, as I said, impossible to come out on 27. The cases got out of the Cust. H. to the binder on the 23rd only and had to be recollated as American binders will take no risks on your collating and I am only waiting the binding to go away.

I will bring over full details of other matters and so will not go into it now, except to observe that no contract has yet been made with a bookseller as agent, since Mr. Lovell advised me to have a copy in hand before I went to see about that.

I have selected as colours for cover dark brown and dark blue. I cannot with my limited help attend to all the un ... [word illegible] work, and so have agreed with the binder that he is to wrap up some 300 copies ready for Fullerton to send out.[94]

In the meantime, as we saw at the outset of this account, Volume I of *The Secret Doctrine* was issued on 20 October 1888, and was mailed to the advance subscribers. The Theosophical Publishing Company, Ltd., London; William Quan Judge, New York; and the Manager of *The Theosophist*, Adyar, Madras, were the joint publishers whose names appear on the title page.[95]

In regard to a later appearance of Volume II, the fact is confirmed from several sources. *Le Lotus* of Paris (Vol. III, Oct.-Nov. 1888, p. 512) says that Vol. II of the *S.D.* should appear in the first days of December 1888. *The Path* (Vol. III, November 1888, p. 268) states over the signature of Mr Judge that the work will be issued from his office on November 1st, and that Vol. II will appear about the end of November. In the following month (p. 298) it says that Vol. I was sent out on November 3rd, and that Vol. II will probably reach subscribers at about the same time as the December 1888 *Path*. In its January 1889 issue (p. 330), however, it speaks of delays that have occurred again, and promises Vol. II before the January *Path* reaches the subscribers.

In November 1888, *The Theosophist* (Vol. X, p. 69) published parts of the 'Proem' of the *S.D.* and some of the stanzas, from advance sheets of Vol. I supplied for that purpose by request. The Editor expected the work to be published almost immediately.

In December 1888, *The Theosophist* published an advertisement of H.P.B's new work and said:

---

[94] Ibid., pp. 133-34

[95] It has been erroneously stated by various writers that *The Secret Doctrine* was printed by the H.P.B. Press in London. This is contrary to facts. There was no such Press in 1888. It was organized in 1890, for which purpose James Morgan Pryse, a printer by profession, came over from New York where he had organized the Aryan Press for Mr Judge.

The splendid work ... is at last published simultaneously in London and New York, and Indian subscribers should receive their copies by the middle of December. The first English edition of 500 copies was exhausted before the day of publication, and a second is preparing. The Manager of *The Theosophist* is appointed the General Agent for India and can supply a few extra copies of the first Edition to those who apply at once. ... There is a copious Index and a Glossary to explain difficult terms used.[96]

It is obvious that the writer of this advertisement meant a second 'printing' instead of a second edition. As he had not yet seen the Index, he had no way of knowing how poor it would be. As to the Glossary, we are at a loss to explain what the reference is supposed to mean, as no such glossary was included in either of the Volumes of the *S.D.* No definite information is available as to why no glossary was included, but Judge, writing to C.H. Whitaker, 11 January 1889, suggests that it probably was found too expensive to produce one.[97] It is conceivable also that material for such a glossary was later used both in *The Key to Theosophy* and in *The Theosophical Glossary*.

As the original 500 copies of Volume I became exhausted at once, another printing was urgently required. This was done from the same type, and hardly any corrections were made at the time. A careful comparison of the first bound copy, which belonged to R. Harte, with copies of this second printing shows that most typographical errors in the one are also present in the other.[98] This should conclusively establish the fact that what is often erroneously called the 'second edition'—even to the extent of having these words printed on the binding—was nothing but a second 'printing' or 'run'.

CONCERNING VOLUMES THREE AND FOUR OF 'THE SECRET DOCTRINE'

We have to examine now, as impartially and objectively as possible, the subject of Volumes III and IV of *The Secret Doctrine*, which has given rise to much controversy through the years.

We shall consider first H.P.B.'s own statements on this subject; they are not many.

---

[96] Vol. X, Suppl. to December 1888, p. xxx a.

[97] *Practical Occultism*, p. 139.

[98] A few minor inaccuracies were rectified: the faulty folio 287 in Vol. I were corrected; the missing folio 2 in Vol. II was restored; and the incomplete folio 26 in the same volume was restored to 626. Curiously enough, folio 7 in Vol. I is entirely missing in the second printing. Folio 60 of Vol. I is missing in both printings; folio 263 in Vol. II is lacking the initial 2 in both printings.

The first, chronologically is of 3 April 1888, and consists of but a few words to the effect that

The MSS. of the first three volumes is now ready for the press.[99]

The next set of six separate statements may very well be of approximately the same date, although we become aware of them only in October and December 1888, in the published volumes of *The Secret Doctrine*. They are as follows:

A large quantity of material has already been prepared, dealing with the history of occultism as contained in the lives of the great Adepts of the Āryan Race, and showing the bearing of occult philosophy upon the conduct of life, as it is and as it ought to be. Should the present volumes meet with a favourable reception, no effort will be spared to carry out the scheme of the work in its entirety. The third volume is entirely ready; the fourth almost so.[100]

Such a point ... cannot be offered to them in these two volumes. But if the reader has patience ... then he will find all this in Volume III of this work.[101]

There is no space to describe these 'fires' ... though we may attempt to do so if the third and fourth volumes of this work are ever published.[102]

In Volume III of this work (the said volume and the IVth being almost ready) a brief history of all the great adepts ... will be given ... Volume IV will be almost entirely devoted to Occult teachings.[103]

Even the mode of divination through 'the idol of the moon' is the same as practiced by David, Saul, and the High Priests of the Jewish Tabernacle by means of the Theraphim. In Volume III, Part II, of this present work, the practical methods of such ancient divination will be found.[104]

These two volumes only constitute the work of a pioneer ... so that these two volumes should form for the student a fitting prelude for Volumes III and IV ... it entirely depends upon the reception with which Volumes I and II will meet at the hands of Theosophists and Mystics, whether these last two volumes will ever be published, though they are almost completed.[105]

The next allusion by H.P.B. is contained in the transcription of the discussion at the Blavatsky Lodge, London, held 31 January 1889, in which H.P.B. said that an

---

[99] H.P.B.'s letter to the second Annual Convention of the Theosophical Society, American Section, held in Chicago, Ill., on 22 and 23 April 1888. The letter was written from London and addressed to William Quan Judge, General Secretary.

[100] Vol. I, Preface, the first paragraph. [101] Vol. I, pp. xxxix-xl.

[102] Vol. II, p. 106. [103] Vol. II, p. 437.

[104] Vol. II, p. 455. [105] Vol. II, pp. 797-98.

> ... additional two volumes of the *Secret Doctrine* would be required to explain all the Hierarchies ...

and that:

> Fuller details on this subject [Seventh Round, Planetary Spirits] have already been written in the third volume of the *Secret Doctrine*.[106]

In a letter written by H.P.B. from London to Judge N.D. Khandalavala and dated 21 November 1889, she says that by leaving India she has

> ... been able to write my *S.D.*, 'Key' and 'Voice' and prepared two more volumes of the S. Doctrine, which I could never have done in the turbulent psychic atmosphere of India.[107]

In February 1890, in a letter written by H.P.B. to her sister in Russia, we are given a completely different slant on the volumes under consideration:

> It is easy for him [the physician] to speak, but all the same I must put the third volume of the *Secret Doctrine* in order, and fourth—hardly begun yet, too ...[108]

The last and the longest statement is contained in H.P.B.'s article entitled 'The Negators of Science', the first part of which appeared in the pages of *Lucifer* (Vol. VIII, no.44) in April 1891, just a few weeks before her death. As she speaks in it of *The Secret Doctrine* as having been out for two years already, it is likely that the article was written sometime in the winter of 1890-91. Her words are as follows:

> Two years ago, the writer promised in *The Secret Doctrine*, Vol. II, p.798, a third and even a fourth volume of that work. This third volume (now almost ready) treats of the ancient Mysteries of Initiation, gives sketches—from the esoteric standpoint—of many of the most famous and historically known philosophers and hierophants (everyone of whom is set down by the Scientists as an *imposter*), from the archaic down to the Christian era, and traces the teachings of all these sages to one and the same source of all knowledge and science...the esoteric doctrine of WISDOM-RELIGION. No need our saying that from the esoteric and legendary materials used in the forthcoming work, its statements and conclusions differ greatly and often clash irreconcilably with the data given by almost all the English and German Orientalists...Now the main point of Volume III of *The Secret Doctrine* is to

---

[106] *Transactions of the Blavatsky Lodge of The Theosophical Society*, Part I, 1890; meeting of January 1889, pp. 39 and 42. *Collected Writings*, Vol. X, pp. 340 and 344.

[107] Transcribed from the original in the Adyar Archives.

[108] *The Path*, New York, Vol. X, December 1895, p. 268.

prove, by tracing and explaining the *blinds* in the woks of ancient Indian, Greek, and other philosophers of note, and also in all the ancient Scriptures—the presence of an uninterrupted esoteric allegorical method and symbolism; to show, as far as lawful, that with the keys of interpretation as taught in the Eastern Hindoo-Buddhistic Canon of Occultism, the *Upanishads*, the *Purānās*, the *Sūtras*, the Epic poems of India and Greece, the Egyptian *Book of the Dead*, the Scandinavian *Eddas*, as well as the Hebrew *Bible*, and even the classical writings of Initiates (such as Plato, among others)—all, from first to last, yield a meaning quite different from their dead letter texts. [109]

As regards the President-Founder, Col. H. S. Olcott, his references to later volumes are of such a general character that they can hardly be taken in any definite meaning at all. In a letter to H.P.B. dated 19 January 1886, he made the suggestion of splitting 'the entire work into *four* volumes', [110] at a time when the division of the material into volumes had not yet been decided.

At the Annual Convention at Adyar, held December 27-28, 1886, he volunteered a guess that H.P.B.'s forthcoming work 'will probably extend to five volumes,' [111] and also made the announcement that 'the entire MSS. of the first of five volumes' was in his hands. [112]

Exactly one year later, speaking at the Annual Convention of 27- 28 Dec. 1887, he said that 'during the past twelve months she [H.P.B.] has sent me the MSS. of four out of the probable five volumes.' [113]

These pronouncements had all been made at a time when no one knew at either end of the line just exactly how the entire material would be finally divided or systematized.

In addition to the above, we have a few other scattered statements by some of the early workers.

We have already seen that Countess Wachtmeister had heard it said (most likely by H.P.B. herself) that *The Secret Doctrine* 'would consist when complete of four volumes'. [114] At the time, she was quite new in the work, having just met H.P.B.

Bertram Keightley, writing to F. K. Gaboriau, editor of *Le Lotus,* 1 June 1887, states that: 'les trois premiers volumes sont prêts' [the first three volumes are ready]. [115]

---

[109] *Lucifer*, Vol. VIII, April 1891, pp. 94-95.

[110] *The Letters of H. P. Blavatsky to A. P. Sinnett*, Letter No. CLXVII, p. 326.

[111] *The Theosophist*, Vol. VIII, Suppl. to January 1887, pp. xx- xxi.

[112] Ibid., p. xlvii.   [113] Ibid., Vol. IX, Suppl. to January, 1888, p. xviii.

[114] *Reminiscences*, etc., p. 23   [115] *Le Lotus*, Paris. Vol. I, June 1887, pp. 216-19

5

A somewhat more definite statement is made by W.Q. Judge who, in a letter to Chas. H. Whitaker, dated 30 June 1888, writes:

> ...2 vols. of Sec. Doct. complete all that will now come out and not five. Any other vol. will be additional. The 3rd vol. is of practical magic and will not, I think, be issued, since neither English nor American people are ready for it but might drop into Black Magic! [116]

After the publication of the two volumes of H.P.B.'s *magnum opus*, an anonymous writer reviewing Dr Anna Bonus Kingsford's work, *Clothed with the Sun* (London: George Redway, 1889), seems to be strongly impressed with the fact that:

> ...to crown all, she [Kingsford] gives in the remarkable passages on pages 127 and 128 an account of the composition of the Gospels in the library of Alexandria which tallies accurately with what Madame Blavatsky wrote three years ago in the third volume of the 'Secret Doctrine' which is not yet published.[117]

It should be stated at this point that no such account in the words of H.P.B. occurs anywhere in her known writings.

On 29 April 1889, Dr Archibald Keightley is reported to have said the following in an interview with a reporter of the New York *Times:*

> The third volume of *The Secret Doctrine* is in manuscript ready to be given to the printers. It will consist mainly of a series of sketches of the great occultists of all ages, and is a most wonderful and fascinating work. The fourth volume, which is to be largely hints on the subject of practical occultism, has been outlined, but not yet written. It will demonstrate what occultism really is, and show how the popular conception of it has been outraged and degraded by fraudulent pretenders to its mysteries, who have, for greed of gain or other base purposes, falsely claimed possession of the secret knowledge. This exposure will necessitate its being brought sharply to date as an historical record, so that the actual work of writing it will not be commenced until we are about ready to bring it forth.[118]

We cannot lay too much trust in the record of a newspaper interview which usually distorts more than it reports; it would also be difficult to understand how any kind of work could be written at the same time as published or 'brought forth'. So we should not give too much attention to this statement, even though it points out the fact that *some* of the sections published later in the 'Volume III' of 1897 had been written as early as 1888 and possibly even 1886.

---

[116] *Practical Occultism*, Pasadena, Calif., 1951, p. 94.

[117] *Lucifer*, Vol. IV, August 1889, p. 521. In the London, 1937 (or 3rd) ed. of Dr Kingsford's work, the passage is in Chapter 32, pp. 80-84.

[118] Reprinted in *The Theosophist*, Vol. X, July 1889, pp. 594-601.

Claude Falls Wright, writing from London under date of 7 January 1891, says that:

> ...H.P.B. had within the last week or two begun to get together the MSS. (long ago written) for the Third Volume of *The Secret Doctrine;* it will, however, take a good twelve months to prepare for publication.[119]

This, we must bear in mind, was written only four months before H.P.B.'s passing.

At about the same time, namely in February 1891, Mrs Alice Leighton Cleather wrote one of her periodical 'London Letters' which was published in *The Theosophist* (Vol. XII, April, 1891, p. 438) in which she spoke of the new edition of *The Secret Doctrine* already then in preparation, and volunteered the information that 'moreover H.P.B. has already started on Vol. III'.

Many years later, in August 1927, James Morgan Pryse, one of the valuable early workers, a printer by profession, contradicted this assertion. To quote his own words:

> Mrs Cleather, who lived at Harrow, was a frequent visitor at the London Headquarters, but was not a member of the working staff, and some of the news items she gives in the letter [referred to above] are quite inaccurate ... according to Mrs Cleather it was only two months before her death that H.P.B. 'started on Vol.III'—and none of us who were on the Headquarters staff, not even Mr Mead, who edited all her MSS., knew anything about it. In several conversations with H.P.B. which I had, at that very time, concerning her writings, she never mentioned any further work on the S.D....No; H.P.B. did *not* start to write a new volume of the S.D. at that time, when her strength was failing and she had but a few more weeks to live.[120]

In December 1891, H.P.B.'s sister, Vera P. de Zhelihovsky, publishing a biographical essay about H.P.B., said in a footnote that 'the 3rd volume was left by her in MSS. and is being printed now'.[121]

Mr Judge writing in *The Path* in March 1895, on the subject of the famous Prayāga message to the Brāhmanas, said that 'its philosophical and occult references are furthermore confirmed by the manuscript of part of the third volume of *The Secret Doctrine*, not yet printed. ...'[122]

---

[119] *The Path*, New York, Vol. V, February 1891, p. 354.

[120] *The Canadian Theosphist*, Vol. VIII, 15 August 1927, p. 114.

[121] Russkoye Obozreniye (Russian Review), December 1891, p. 603.

[122] Vol IX, p. 431.

An important statement by G.R.S. Mead occurs in his Editorial 'On the Watch-Tower', in the 15 July 1897 issue of *Lucifer* (Vol. XX, No. 119, pp. 353-54). He says:

> One of the substantial misconceptions that H.P.B. laboured under was that she had in hand a sufficient mass of MSS. to make two additional volumes. This was not actually the case. No doubt had she lived she would have carried out her promise, for her custom was to write at least half of the work she was engaged upon as it was going through the press.

He then continues with some critical remarks about 'Volume III' as published in 1897.

Curiously enough, the subject of Volumes III and IV seems to disappear at approximately that time from theosophical journals, to reappear some thirty years later and be discussed again.

It first makes its sudden appearance in the *Hamilton Spectator*, Ontario, Canada, which published 6 October 1926, an interview between Annie Besant and William Mulliss, Managing Editor of that paper, a competent reporter and for ten years a student of *The Secret Doctrine*. The interview took place at Los Angeles, California.

> *Mr Mulliss.* Your critics have insisted that somebody or other has deliberately suppressed the Third and Fourth Volumes of *The Secret Doctrine* to which H.P.B. makes reference in the First Volume of *The Secret Doctrine*. What have you to say to this? Do you regard the Third Volume of your edition of *The Secret Doctrine* entitled 'Occultism' as containing any of the matter intended for the Third and Fourth Volumes?[123]
>
> *Mrs Besant.* I was appointed H.P.B.'s literary executor and the matter from which I compiled the Third Volume of 'Occultism' in *The Secret Doctrine* published under my direction was compiled from a mass of miscellaneous writings found in her desk after her death. These I took under my own charge.
>
> *Mr Mulliss.* Did Mead help you in the compilation of these articles?
>
> *Mrs Besant.* No. The papers came absolutely under my own hand and Mead had nothing to do with them.
>
> *Mr Mulliss.* Well, what about the material for the Third and Fourth Volumes?
>
> *Mrs Besant.* I never saw them and do not know what became of them.[124]

It should be pointed out, in connection with the above excerpt, that there exists no documentary evidence whatever about Mrs Annie Besant having been

---

[123] Reference is here to the Volume published in 1897.

[124] Quoted in the *O.E. Library Critic*, June 1938.

appointed literary executor of H.P.B.'s will. She appointed Col. H.S. Olcott and Damodar K. Mavalankar as her executors; as the latter had withdrawn to Tibet, the Colonel took charge of things at H.P.B.'s death. Her will was filed at Adyar and its contents are well known. As far as English law is concerned, a literary executor can be appointed only in a will. If the legal executor (Olcott) appointed anyone else to take charge of H.P.B.'s papers, etc., this would not give such a person any power whatever in law, all control remaining in the named executors.

Thirteen years later, Basil Crump, then at Ranchi, India, writing in *The Canadian Theosophist*,[125] tells his readers that:

> A very important piece of evidence throwing an entirely new light on the mysterious disappearance of Vols. III and IV of *The Secret Doctrine* has lately been revealed to the Blavatsky Association by an elderly gentleman, a devoted admirer of Madame Blavatsky, who knew Mr Thomas Green, one of the well-known early workers who helped with the printing at the H.P.B. Press in London before and after H.P.B.'s death. Before he died Mr Green told this gentleman, who prefers to withold his name, that he worked at the London Headquarters for some time and was paid to set up the type of Vol. III and part of Vol. IV of *The Secret Doctrine*. The proofs of Vol. III were passed by H.P.B. shortly before her death and Mr Green was just going to press with them when he received orders from her to break up the type, also such portions of Vol. IV as had already been set. ... That she gave orders for the type to be broken up makes it practically certain that she also destroyed the MSS.... Belonging to a leading firm of solicitors, his [Green's] legal training was most useful, and I as a member of the Bar learned to respect his integrity.

As might have been expected, James Morgan Pryse, then at Los Angeles, read this statement with undisguised surprise and sent a communication to *The Canadian Theosophist* in reply to it. We quote some pertinent excerpts from this communication:

> Extraordinary! Mr Green was not a printer, did not learn to set type, and was never connected with any printing office but the H.P.B. Press. He assisted me in the pressroom and kept the books. He had no part in the management, and never handled any 'copy', as that was always given to me as manager.... He had nothing to do with the printing until I took him in as my assistant when the printing plant was enlarged, quite a while *after* H.P.B. discarded her wornout body. ... 'The proofs of Vol. III were passed by H.P.B. shortly before her death.' During all that time I was at the Headquarters and spent nearly every evening with H.P.B. in the drawing-room

---

[125] Vol. XX, 15 April 1939, pp. 39-40.

where she wrote and conversed with members of the staff, she read no proofs of the
S.D. If she had done so all of us would have known it. Mr Green was never a
member of the staff.... [As to breaking up the type, etc.] At that time Mr Green was
clerking in a law office and had had no experience in the printing business. To set up
a volume of the S.D. and keep the type standing would require thousands of
pounds—say two tons—of type, leads and galleys. In printing the S.D. [the 1897
Volume, he means] I used an eight-ton Cottrell press and ran about twenty tons of
paper through it each year. Where did Mr Green keep such an outfit? ... Thomas
Green, who worked faithfully with me for several years, was thoroughly honourable
and truthful. He could not possibly have told the ridiculous lies which the 'elderly
gentleman' sneaking behind anonymity, attributes to him. He could not 'before he
died', or after passing on to the other world, have uttered those gross falsehoods.[126]

So much for Mr Pryse. While his explanation concerning Mr Green
and the circumstances prevailing at Headquarters at the time when Mr Pryse
was working there have the weight of an eyewitness account, we
should not overlook the obvious fact that Mr Pryse came to London only in the
autumn of 1890. By discrediting the story of the 'elderly gentleman', as it
seems reasonable to do, no factual information is given as to the existence or
non-existence of any manuscript from H.P.B.'s pen prior to Mr Pryse's arrival
in London.

In connection with Mr Green's alleged disclosure, we have a
communication from E.T. Sturdy, a member of the Inner Group at the time,
and a devoted worker of the early days, who, in a letter to *The Canadian
Theosophist* [127] supports Mr Pryse's statement regarding any further MSS. and
says that Bertram Keightley wrote to him in confirmation of what Mr Pryse had
said. He adds:

Incidentally Mr J.M. Watkins, who lived in the closest mutual regard with
Mr Green, has remarked to me that he considers it as the height of improbability that
his close friend of so many years should have made any statement to another person
(anonymous!) upon so weighty a subject and not have mentioned it through long
years of intimacy to him.

In considering this problem, we can discard the unsupported story relayed
by an 'elderly gentleman' about Thomas Green and Volume III. We can also
set aside all statements by Col. Olcott, because, at the time he mentioned more
than two volumes, no division into volumes had yet been made, and it was
altogether too early to speculate as to how many volumes H.P.B.'s work would
contain.

---

[126] *The Canadian Theosophist*, Vol. XX, May 1939, pp. 73-77.   [127] Ibid., p. 152.

The testimony of the Keightleys is one of the most interesting in this respect. Their accounts make it clear that a considerable amount of material—some of it dealing with the lives of Adepts and Occultists—was intended to be the First Part of *The Secret Doctrine* but was set aside and not used when another distribution of the text had been decided upon. After they had finished their task, they tied up the manuscript, 'complete *as it was*', making 'a strong sealed parcel of it'.[128] This would most likely indicate that the *unused part* was in that package also.

It is possible that *some* of the unused material contained therein (or copies thereof) was later incorporated into the so-called 'Volume III' published in 1897 and consisting of miscellaneous essays and articles. There seems to be nothing against this supposition. As a matter of record a few facts are available in support of it. One of them is H.P.B.'s reference on page 11 of the Proem to *The Secret Doctrine*, where she suggests that the reader should 'see Book III, *Gupta-Vidyā* and the *Zohar*'. This is obviously a reference to her projected Volume III, and may be connected with the *unused* material set aside by the Keightleys. Among the various sections of the so-called 'Volume III' of 1897, this subject is discussed in Sections XX-XXV. Another reference to 'Book III' is on page 76 of Volume I, and deals with Fohat. Still another is in a footnote on page 52 of Vol. I, where H.P.B. mentions a 'subsequent Volume' in which 'the Mystery about Buddha' may be explained more fully. This reference may very well be directly connected with Sections XLIII-XLVIII of the so-called 'Volume III' of 1897, in which the subject is explained at considerable length. The material of the above-mentioned sections in 'Volume III' may have been drawn from the *unused* text we have been discussing, or copies of some of that material may have existed elsewhere among H.P.B.'s papers.

This, however, does not exhaust the problem, and we have to consider at this point H.P.B.'s own testimony.

As far as that testimony is concerned, the strongest evidence for the existence, at one time or another, of material which has not come down to us, is her letter to A.P. Sinnett dated March 3rd, most likely of 1886, which has already been quoted.[129]

In it she speaks of an 'enormous Introductory Chapter, or *Preamble*, Prologue, call it what you will'. Every section thereto is said to begin with 'a

---

[128] Bertram Keightley, *Reminiscences of H.P.B.*, 1932, p. 13.

[129] *The Letters of H.P. Blavatsky to A.P. Sinnett*, p. 195.

page of translation from the Book of *Dzyan* and the Secret Book of "Maitreya Buddha" *Champai chhos Nga*[130] (in prose, not the five books in verse known, which are a blind).'

She gives Sinnett a bird's-eye view of the partial contents of that introductory chapter, and speaks of it as 'the *short* survey of the forthcoming Mysteries in the text—which covers 300 pages of foolscap'.[131]

Geoffrey A. Barborka, writing on this subject in one of his invaluable works,[132] discusses this letter and points out a number of important facts. H.P.B.'s 'Prologue', as described by her, is certainly not the 'Introductory' published in Volume I of *The Secret Doctrine*. The published Introductory does not correspond to the description given by H.P.B. to Sinnett; it is not divided into sections, and consists of only 31 printed pages.

The proem of the published work is not divided into sections either, and occupies only 24 pages.

No citations from, or references to, *Champai chhos Nga* are to be found anywhere in *The Secret Doctrine*.

It should be noted that the material which H.P.B. speaks of was intended, possibly with other texts on the subject of the Mystery-Schools, to be in Volume I of her *magnum opus*. The Keightleys, however, rearranged the manuscript, with H.P.B.'s consent and approval, and the division of the work into two volumes, dealing with cosmogenesis and anthropogenesis respectively, was the result of this decision.

It is also important to remember that H.P.B.'s description of this material in her letter to Sinnett does not tally with any of the miscellaneous material gathered together and published in 1897 under the rather misleading title of 'Secret Doctrine, Volume III'. Nor does the latter contain any material dealing with the early Christian centuries, the compilation of the Gospels in the library of Alexandria, and collateral subjects, as has already been mentioned above. Moreover, it does not contain anything on the subject of Dhyāni-Buddhas and Planetary Spirits in charge of the various Globes of our Planetary Chain, and

---

[130] This compound Tibetan term is derived from *champai*, meaning whole, unimpaired; *chhos*, doctrine; and *ngang*, essentiality. It can therefore be translated as 'the whole doctrine in its essentiality'.

[131] Paper in sheets measuring approximately 13x16 or 17 inches; so called from the water-mark of a fool's cap and bells used by old papermakers. Three hundred pages of foolscap would represent a great deal of material, running into several hundred pages when printed.

[132] *H.P. Blavatsky, Tibet and Tulku*. Adyar: Theosophical Publishing House, 1966, pp. 186-88; 3rd printing, 1975.

their condition during the 'minor pralayas' or obscurations, 'fuller details on this subject [having] already been written in the third volume of *The Secret Doctrine*', to quote H.P.B.'s own words.[133]

When we bear in mind that H.P.B. speaks of 300 pages of foolscap, it is obvious that we are dealing here with a considerable amount of material, running, if printed, into several hundred pages.

The question may well arise as to whether the Keightleys included these 300 pages of foolscap in the package of manuscripts which they tied together and gave back to H.P.B. who eventually took it with her to 19 Avenue Road, St. John's Wood, London N.W.

When the Keightleys' own story is carefully analysed, the deduction seems warranted that the material intended by H.P.B. at first for Volume I was neither rearranged by them nor typed, but merely set aside. What has become of it?

Rather fantastic legends have been set on foot through the years about the withdrawal or the alleged destruction of Volumes III and IV of *The Secret Doctrine*. It has even been asserted by some that the manuscript has been purposely hidden away and will be given out to the world when the time is ripe. It is likely that the sponsors of this idea do not realize that the mysterious manuscript, if produced and published, will be what is known as 'dated', with many outdated references to former scientific facts and those dealing with ancient scriptures and mythologies which have since been carefully reconsidered by scholars, and often radically altered in the light of subsequent discoveries. This, of course, would not affect the validity of any actual occult teachings involved.

Nevertheless, it would be foolish to disregard statements made by reliable people who knew H.P.B. personally and were on close terms with her. One such was Dr Herbert Coryn, a personal pupil of H.P.B. in the London days, who later in life resided for many years and passed away at Point Loma. To quote Geoffrey A. Barborka:

> In discussing the publication of *The Secret Doctrine* with Dr Herbert Coryn at Point Loma, California, the information was volunteered that he himself had seen the manuscript of H.P.B.'s third volume on her desk. He was definitely not referring to what was published after H.P.B.'s passing [in 1897], for Dr Coryn was well aware of what the posthumous printed volume contained. The doctor was not able to say what had become of the manuscript which he saw.[134]

---

[133] *Transactions of the Blavatsky Lodge* Part I, p. 42.
[134] G.A. Barborka, op.cit., p. 188.

It is evident from the various pronouncements quoted, that no outright positive or negative answer can be made to the oft- repeated question whether a completed manuscript of Volumes III and IV ever existed. The subject is open to further discussion, and it is probable that speculation about it will continue.

In all ages, and in all lands, the belief has existed that a divine degree of knowledge is possible to human beings under certain conditions; and, as a corollary to this, the conviction has dwelt in the hearts of the people that living men exist who possess this knowledge. In ancient days, some of this higher knowledge was taught in the Mystery-Schools, traces of which have been found among all the nations of the earth. In more modern days, its existence has been suspected by intuitive thinkers who called it by various names such as 'Wisdom-Religion', the 'Gnosis', or the 'Esoteric Philosophy'.

It is to the elucidation of the teachings of that 'Wisdom-Religion' that the two volumes of *The Secret Doctrine* are devoted. In the words of H.P. Blavatsky herself:

> These truths are in no sense put forward as a *revelation*; nor does the author claim the position of a revealer of mystic lore, now made public for the first time in the world's history ... this work is a partial statement of what she herself has been taught by more advanced students, supplemented, in a few details only, by the results of her own study and observations. ...
>
> It is needless to explain that this book is not the Secret Doctrine in its entirety, but a select number of fragments of its fundamental tenets ...
>
> The aim of this work may be thus stated: to show that Nature is not 'a fortuitous concurrence of atoms', and to assign to man his rightful place in the scheme of the Universe; to rescue from degradation the archaic truths which are the basis of all religions; and to uncover, to some extent, the fundamental unity from which they all sprang; finally, to show that the occult side of Nature has never been approached by the Science of modern civilization.
>
> If this is in any degree accomplished, the writer is content. It is written in the service of humanity, and by humanity and the future generations it must be judged. Its author recognizes no inferior court of appeal. Abuse she is accustomed to; calumny she is daily acquainted with; at slander she smiles in silent contempt. [Preface.]

With this outspoken send-off, the most important literary production from the pen of H.P. Blavatsky became public property.

The first of the two volumes of *The Secret Doctrine* is primarily concerned with the evolution of the cosmos, the awakening of Septenary Hierarchies to a new Cosmic Day after a period of latency, and the growth and development of Planetary Chains.

A most important INTRODUCTORY establishes the setting for what follows. The Secret Doctrine is declared to have been 'the universally diffused religion of the ancient and prehistoric world', and the work itself, far from being a mere treatise, 'or a series of vague theories', is said to 'contain all that can be given out to the world in this [the XIXth] century'. A prophetic statement is made to the effect that 'in Century the Twentieth some disciple more informed, and far better fitted, may be sent by the Masters of Wisdom to give final and irrefutable proofs that there exists a Science called *Gupta-Vidyā*. ...'

Next comes the PROEM which embodies the now famous Three Fundamental Propositions of the Secret Doctrine, elaborated and expanded in the 'Summing Up' section (Vol. I, pp. 269-99). The skeleton of Volume I is formed by seven stanzas translated from the secret *Book of Dzyan*, the original of which is written in the sacred language of the Initiates—the Senzar. The stanzas and their commentaries and explanations form Part I of this first volume.

Part II is devoted to the elucidation of the fundamental symbols contained in the great religions of the world, and the occult meaning of the hidden ideographs and glyphs.

Part III outlines the contrasting views of science and the Secret Doctrine and meets probable scientific objections by anticipation. This part serves as a connecting link between the two volumes.

The general arrangement of Volume II is similar to that of Volume I. It deals primarily with the evolution of man on this planet, the subject being introduced by 'Preliminary Notes' on the Archaic Stanzas and the four prehistoric continents.

Part I is based on twelve stanzas from the *Book of Dzyan* describing the gradual evolution of humanity through many occult stages, the origin of the lower kingdoms of nature, the submergence of ancient continents, and presents a panoramic view of bygone civilizations.

Part II deals with the archaic symbolism of the world-religions, with special emphasis on the sevenfold and quaternary classification of elements and forces.

Part III contrasts again the teachings of the wisdom-religion with those of current science, mainly in the domain of anthropology and geology.

Having written some 1,500 pages on these recondite and fascinating subjects, H.P. Blavatsky concludes by saying that 'these two volumes had to serve as a PROLOGUE, and prepare the reader's mind for those which shall now follow'. With the traditional modesty of a true disciple she points out that her main concern 'was simply to prepare the soil. This, we trust, we have done'. Having opened before the reader's eyes a vision of cosmic grandeur, and stretched his mental and spiritual capacities to a far-flung horizon of evolving systems, interpenetrating hierarchies and limitless cycles of evolution, she closes by saying:

> These two volumes only constitute the work of a pioneer who has forced his way into the well-nigh impenetrable jungle of the virgin forests of the Land of the Occult. A commencement has been made to fell and uproot the deadly upas trees of superstition, prejudice, and conceited ignorance, so that these two volumes should form for the student a fitting prelude for Volumes III and IV. Until the rubbish of the ages is cleared away from the minds of the Theosophists to whom these volumes are dedicated, it is impossible that the more practical teaching contained in the Third Volume should be understood. Consequently, it entirely depends upon the reception with which Volumes I and II will meet at the hands of Theosophists and Mystics, whether these last two volumes will ever be published, though they are *almost* completed.

From the various documents quoted in the present outline, it is abundantly clear that *The Secret Doctrine* is actually a great deal more than just an explanation of, and a running commentary on, certain stanzas translated from the *Book of Dzyan*. Throughout its pages there are a great many passages which begin with such expressions as: 'Occultism teaches', 'the Secret Doctrine states', 'the Esoteric Philosophy affirms', 'Occult Science declares', followed by a succinct exposition of certain occult truths expressed in direct and unequivocal language. When such passages are linked together it becomes obvious that *The Secret Doctrine*, in its essential framework, is a comprehensive outline of the heretofore secret science or philosophy of occultism, publicly given out by two or more Initiates of the Brotherhood of Adepts through the intermediary of their direct messenger, H.P. Blavatsky.

Its text contains several different yet interrelated levels, from the scientific arguments and philosophical dissertations of H.P. Blavatsky as a student of mystical lore, to the inspired ideas, penetrating thoughts, and prophetic statements of an initiated occultist—H.P.B., and beyond these, to the lofty pronouncements and stirring passages directly from the minds of higher occultists which, at times, resound like the peal of organ music in the vastness of space. Unless this complex scheme of the work is grasped, the real nature of *The Secret Doctrine* will not be understood.

Some students, impressed by the vast amount of collateral information contained in this work, and dealing mainly with supporting evidence drawn from various religions, philosophies, and mythologies the world over, have imagined *The Secret Doctrine* to be a syncretistic work wherein a multitude of seemingly unrelated teachings and ideas are cleverly woven together to form a more or less coherent whole. Nothing could be farther from the truth than this.

H.P.B.'s *magnum opus* is intended to present a wholly coherent outline of an ageless doctrine, a system of thought based upon occult facts and universal truths inherent in nature and which are as specific and definite as any mathematical proposition. The teaching of that system as a whole cannot be deduced from, or found in, any of the known exoteric religious or philosophical schools of ancient or more recent times, although separate ideas and single tenets can be occasionally found or hinted at, in the works of ancient writers, suggesting the existence of a parent doctrine carefully hidden from view.

The stupendous cosmogenesis and anthropogenesis presented for our consideration and study are completely *sui generis*; they are not copied from any of the world-scriptures, nor are they pieced together from a number of them. They challenge investigation as the most extraordinary literary problem of our age. Unless H.P.B.'s own explanation concerning their source is accepted, no other explanation is of the slightest value.

Already as early as 1883, H.P.B., while discussing various conflicting views about Buddhism on the part of western orientalists, took occasion to point out that:

> The only way in which they will solve the problems raised, will be by paying attention to the direct teachings of the Secret Doctrine which are now being given out to the world through the columns of this Magazine (*The Theosophist*) for the first time in the history of the subject.[135]

The Secret Doctrine is the first major work in *several thousand years* which is intended to, and actually does, outline in a consecutive and coherent manner the foundation principles of that universal occult doctrine—the *Brahma-Vidyā*, the *Gupta-Vidyā*, the *Gnosis Pneumatikos*—which was the original knowledge of the *Mānasaputras*, who brought it to nascent mankind in this Round and left it in the care of its then highest exponents as a perennial fountainhead of spiritual truths.

It should, of course, be borne in mind that *The Secret Doctrine* outlines but a small portion of that universal occult tradition which in H.P.B.'s own words is 'the accumulated Wisdom of the Ages'. It is but the lifting of a corner of the

---

[135] *The Theosophist,* Vol IV, May 1883, p. 182.

mystic veil which hides the higher degrees or levels of this knowledge. Hence it would be foolish for anyone to imagine that H.P.B.'s work is the last word of that knowledge; it is but the general outline of some of the basic principles thereof.

In the light of existing evidence, both published and traditional, it is therefore obvious that the principal sources of *The Secret Doctrine*—and this applies to many other portions of H.P.B.'s literary output—are collectively the Brotherhood of Adepts whose direct messenger she was, and, individually, two or more of the Initiates belonging to this Brotherhood, and who chose to unveil in our present era a certain portion of their traditionally hidden knowledge for the benefit of those who were ready to receive it.

The vehicle—man-made and therefore imperfect—which was to serve for the widespread dissemination of these truths was the Theosophical Society, founded in 1875 on direct orders of the Brotherhood. In spite of its many failures and shortcomings it still remains the best exponent, in this world of ignorance and confusion, of the ageless teachings of the *Gupta-Vidyā*. To be true to its original intent, faithful to its foundation principles and pregnant with truth for the sake of the future, it is imperative that it should preserve inviolate that body of 'direct teachings of the Secret Doctrine' which have been entrusted to its care by the real Founders of the movement—the Adepts of the trans-Himalayan Brotherhood. We as students and workers in that movement have a duty to perform and a mandate to carry out, namely, to preserve the purity of that system of thought and the coherence of that body of teaching which have been handed down to us as a spiritual heritage by those who chose to place them into our hands.

BORIS DE ZIRKOFF
Editor

TRANSLATIONS OF 'THE SECRET DOCTRINE' INTO OTHER LANGUAGES

Die Geheimlehre. Die Vereinigung von Wissenschaft, Religion und Philosophic. German translation by Robert Froebe, Dr Phil., based on the Third and Revised Edition, London 1893. Leipzig: Verlag von Wilhelm Friedrick [1899]. Three volumes. Facsimile reproduction by J.J. Couvreur, The Hague, Holland, 1969, in six volumes, incl. Index.

De Geheime Leer. De Synthese van Wetenschap, Godsdienst en Wijsbegeerten. Facsimile reproduction of the Dutch translation by W.B. Fricke issued by the Theosofische Vereniging of the Netherlands in 1931. J.J. Couvreur: Algemene Boekencentrale en Antiquariaat, The Hague, Holland, 1968. Two volumes in one. Translation based on the original edition of 1888.

Den Hemliga Läran. Sammanfattning af Vetenskap, Religion och Filosofi. Swedish translation by Dr Phil. F. Kellberg from the 1893 edition. Stockholm, 1895-98.

Den Hemmelige Laere. En Syntese af Videnskab, Religion og Filosofi. Danish translation by Miss Sigrid Møller based on the Adyar edition of 1962. Published by Det Teosofiske Samfund and Strubes Forlag, Copenhagen, 1970-72. Four volumes, covering only the first four books of the Adyar edition.

La Dottrina Segreta: Sintesi della Scienza, della Religione, della Filosofia. Italian translation: Vol. I by Roberto Hack, published in three books, 1943, 1947, 1951, by Fratelli Bocca, Milan, Italy. Translated from the original edition of 1888. About one-half of Vol. II translated by Selma Bedarf from the 1893 edition and published in 1953. The translations contain many errors and need careful editorial corrections.

La Doctrina Secreta: sintesis de la cienecia, la religión y la filosofia. Spanish translation from the Third Edition of 1893. Published by Editorial Kier, Sociedad de la Responsibilidad Limitada, Telcahuano, 1075, Buenos Aires, Argentine. First ed., in six books, 1943-46; 2nd ed., 1957; 6th ed., 1976. Checked by a group of members of the Theosophical Society in Spain.

La Doctrine Secrète. Synthèse de la Science, de la Religion et de la Philosophie. French translation by a group of students based on the Third and Revised edition of 1893, and further revised in accordance with the 1938 Adyar edition. The six volumes do not include the index-volume, and their publication dates cover the years 1961-1976. Éditions Adyar, 4 Square Rapp, 75007 Paris.

A Doutrina Secreta. Protuguese translation prepared by Shr. Raymundo Mendes Sobral, on the basis of the original edition of 1888. Published by Editora Civilização Brasileria S.A., Rio de Janeiro, Brazil, 1975. Six volumes totaling 1,821 pages. Due to very rapid sales, a second edition was planned for 1978.

Taynaya Doktrina. Sintez nauki, religii i filosofii. Russian translation of the English original, made by Madame Helena de Roerich, in collaboration with her husband Nikolay Konstantinovich de Roerich. Translation was made from the Third and Revised Edition of 1893, and published at Riga by the Izdevnieciba 'Uguns', Dreilinu iela 15, in 1937. Vol. I, xxiv, 845 pp. ; Vol. II, xviii, 2, 1008 pp. No Index. Bound in light blue. *Extremely scarce.* Some years after its publication most of the edition was destroyed at Riga during revolutionary uprisings. Microfilm of the translation has been deposited in the Adyar Archives, the British Museum and the Library of Congress (Microfilm Slavic 996 BP Mic 59-7087), in 1958. These are positive films from an original negative one.

A Titkos Tanitás. A Tudomány, A Vallás és a filozofia Synthezise. Hungarian translation by Dr Hennyey Vilmos and Szlemenics Mária. Contains only Part I of Volume I, and consists of xv, 350 pp. Foreword about H.P.B. and her work. Published by: M.M., and printed in Budapest, Hungary [no date]. *Scarce.*

Kaghni Vaetabedutian Tasuntatzk. Taknakidootian Dasnergoo Himery. Armenian translation by Torkom Saraydarian, including most of the text. Only a portion of it was privately published in Beirut, Lebanon, in 1969, in a book containing 165 pages and dealing with the Twelve Fundamental Principles of *The Secret Doctrine*.

In addition to the above, a number of foreign translations have been published of *An Abridgement of The Secret Doctrine*, edited by Elizabeth Preston and Christmas Humphreys, and published by The Theosophical Publishing House, London, 1966.